A Sense of Place

Forrest Shreve demonstrating the use of a dendrograph on a saguaro

A Sense of Place

The Life and Work of Forrest Shreve

Janice Emily Bowers

The University of Arizona Press, Tucson

For my parents

THE UNIVERSITY OF ARIZONA PRESS

This book was set in 10/13 Linotron 202 Galliard.
Manufactured in the U.S.A.

Library of Congress Cataloging-in-Publication Data

Bowers, Janice Emily.
A sense of place : the life and work of Forrest Shreve / Janice Emily Bowers.
p. cm.
Bibliography: p.
Includes index.
ISBN 0-8165-1072-5 (alk. paper)
1. Shreve, Forrest. 1878–1950. 2. Plant ecologists—United States—Biography. I. Title.
QK31.S49B68 1988
581.5'092'4—dc19
[B] 88-14014
CIP

British Library Cataloguing in Publication data are available.

Contents

List of Illustrations vii

Preface ix

His Home the Desert 1

Getting Experience 9

A Good Fit All Around 18

The Limbo of Controversy 24

Energy, Push, and Solid Horse Sense 31

Tumamocville 42

The Shifting Panorama 47

Point and Counterpoint 56

Mountain Islands 63

Our Mutual Arbeit 68

A Place in the Sun 78

The Finest Trip 84

A Wider Outlook 91

A Splendid Field for Work 100

Understanding Desert Life 110

A Model and a Classic 124

A Bitter Shock 138

Weaving the Threads 149

Appendix: Common Plant Names and Their Scientific Equivalents 153

Notes to the Chapters 155

Bibliography

Publications of Forrest Shreve 180

Index 185

Illustrations

Photographs

Forrest Shreve demonstrating the use of a dendrograph on a saguaro Frontispiece

Henry and Helen Shreve in Easton, Maryland 3

Forrest Shreve, about age eight 5

The Desert Laboratory in 1911 16

Edith Bellamy, about age twenty 22

Forrest Shreve in the field about 1915 37

The Desert Laboratory pack train in the Santa Catalina Mountains 48

The Shreves, camping in Marshall Gulch, in the Santa Catalina Mountains 49

Forrest Shreve at his desk 92

Shreve's office at the Desert Laboratory 92

Forrest Shreve and daughter Margaret beside the Willys Knight 112

Ferrying across the Río Yaqui 115

Forrest Shreve in the field about 1940 140
The Desert Laboratory staff about 1938 144

Maps

Seven regions of the Sonoran Desert first delineated, named, and described by Forrest Shreve 131
Four major deserts of North America first delineated and described by Forrest Shreve 147

Preface

The story of Forrest Shreve's life is actually many stories, not all of which can be known by the biographer. In the following account, two threads run side by side and occasionally entwine. One is Shreve's development from a promising young student to a mature plant ecologist devoted to seeing "the whole pattern and design of desert life."[1] This story inspires and comforts; we would all like to believe that our lives progress steadily toward ever greater achievement, understanding, and contentment. The second story is less inspiring. It tells of a scientist who made his most innovative contributions when young, who was ahead of his times at the beginning of his career but behind them at the end.

Although I was tempted to present only the progressive story, such a biography would ultimately have failed to deal with the contradictions and thus the reality of Shreve's life. In the end, I have written both, in the belief that taken together they tell a life worth remembering.

Shreve's biographical record is far from complete. His boyhood and youth are poorly documented, and his early years at the Desert

Laboratory, from 1908 to 1925, are only sporadically represented in archival materials. Luckily, the activities of his later years are more fully recorded, partly in correspondence with colleagues and partly in the diaries he kept from 1932 until he died in 1950. Although most of the terse, intermittent entries note mundane events—visitors to his office, repairs to the house or car, family celebrations—they do help to recreate the chronology of those years. Few entries offer a glimpse into his emotional life.

Shreve himself is partly responsible for these gaps. He made no arrangements for the preservation of his papers, and it is simply fortuitous that not all of them were destroyed. Clearly, he had little interest in recording his feelings or in preserving traces of his development as a scientist. No doubt it never occurred to him that these personal matters would one day interest others.

In preparing this biography, I have interviewed in person or by letter many of Shreve's colleagues and friends. Archives I have consulted are those at the University of Arizona Library, which is the major repository for the records of the Desert Laboratory, and the Arizona Heritage Center, which holds the Daniel T. MacDougal correspondence. Additional correspondence and memoranda are located at the Carnegie Institution of Washington.

The joy with which Forrest Shreve's friends shared their memories of him speaks eloquently of his kindness and humanity. I thank each of them: Marjorie Denney, Howard Scott Gentry, Robert R. Humphrey, Thomas D. Mallery, William G. McGinnies, Cornelius H. Muller, and Tad Nichols. I am particularly indebted to Margaret Shreve Conn, Forrest Shreve's daughter, for taking the time and energy to answer many questions during her final illness and for loaning me Shreve's diaries. Eric Ashby, Daniel Axelrod, Rexford Daubenmire, Faurest Davis, Peter C. Duisberg, Frank E. Egler, Mildred Mathias, Rogers McVaugh, Erna R. Turnage, and William A. Turnage shared memories, opinions, and answers of a less personal sort. William G. McGinnies made available correspondence and notes from his history of the Desert Laboratory.

Several librarians and archivists provided valuable help, among them Barbara Callahan, Harvard University; Louis Hieb and his staff, University of Arizona; Anita Karg, Hunt Institute for Botanical Documentation; Lothian Lynas, New York Botanical Garden; James Stimpert, Johns Hopkins University; and Susan Vasquez, Carnegie Institution of Washington.

Through the University of Arizona Foundation, the Tumamoc Hill Committee provided partial funding for this project.

Inevitably, errors of fact and interpretation creep into any biography. I thank the readers of the manuscript, who intercepted many errors and provided invaluable comments, insights, and ideas: Tony L. Burgess, Robert R. Humphrey, Paul S. Martin, Joseph R. McAuliffe, Robert P. McIntosh, Steven P. McLaughlin, Robert Robichaux, and Raymond M. Turner. I am particularly indebted to Robert Robichaux for insights into Shreve's early contributions in physiological ecology and to Joseph McAuliffe and Steven McLaughlin for pointing out recent trends in plant ecology.

Without the initial encouragement of William G. McGinnies and Raymond M. Turner, I would not have had the temerity to write this book, and I am deeply grateful to them for their faith in me.

Finally, I owe a special debt of gratitude to Steven P. McLaughlin, who gave me encouragement, love, and the precious gift of time in which to write.

We need to weave together the separate threads of knowledge about the plants and their natural setting into a close fabric of understanding on which it will be possible to see the whole pattern and design of desert life.

—*Forrest Shreve*

His Home the Desert

"My own home," Forrest Shreve wrote in 1926, "happens to be located on the rocky footslope of a volcanic hill."[1] The roadrunners used his paths as much as he did, he noted, and orioles built nests and raised young within four feet of his windows. Over time, large bushes near his house had perished from drought and new ones had sprung up in their places..

Shreve felt no need to improve the desert around his home. He asked, "Why should the Southwest be ashamed of the things that are its own? Why should we not take pride in the things with which nature has so richly endowed us?"[2] His pleasure in untrammeled nature was not merely a selfish one. The desert was, he wrote, a place in which everyone can "learn to know nature as untouched by man, and to interpret the complex activities of plants, animals, and their physical environment."[3]

When Forrest Shreve wrote these words at the age of forty-seven, he had lived in the desert for nearly two decades. Interpreting the complex activities of its plants and animals had been his major occupation, and avocation, as well. He had published several papers and books on the ecology of desert plants, among them the classic

Vegetation of a Desert Mountain Range as Conditioned by Climatic Factors. His most intensive work was yet to come: his landmark treatise *Vegetation of the Sonoran Desert* and his delineation of the four major deserts of North America. Based on these and the remainder of his oeuvre—some eighty-five papers and books—Shreve would be called "a major student of desert ecology"[4] and "a major contributor to the study of American desert ecology."[5] No ecologist during Shreve's lifetime (and few since) surpassed his knowledge of desert plant ecology.

Paradoxically, this expertise worked against his reputation. Shreve worked in Arizona and Sonora at a time when most American plant ecologists labored in the East and Midwest; since his research dealt primarily with desert plants, his contemporaries assumed his findings had little relevance to theirs. Also, Shreve's thought was at times far in advance of his colleagues',[6] and he was not always given proper credit when ecological thought finally caught up with him.

Nor has Shreve's work been adequately evaluated in recent years; historians have been content to call him a desert ecologist and leave it at that. This label ignores his theoretical contributions, his studies of plant ecology in temperate and tropical zones, and his innovations in physiological ecology, population ecology, and community ecology.

Unluckily for Shreve's posthumous reputation, he was not adept at marketing his ideas. Although many scientists are reluctant to admit it, they are as susceptible to the lures of attractive packaging as any shopper in a department store. The most successful scientists wrap their theories in catchy labels and flashy jargon. Marketing involves not only packaging but promotion as well, and the ability to capitalize on current research fads. All this Shreve failed to do.

This failure, if such it was, arose from Shreve's personality. A modest man, he was little concerned with status or self-glorification. Moreover, he was content to investigate interesting problems without establishing a school of thought, lobbying fellow ecologists, training graduate students, or writing textbooks. He could have extracted ideas from his various works and expressed them in theoretical papers. Instead he remained rooted to the particular—ideas appealed to him largely in their specific application to real places.

Henry and Helen Shreve in Easton, Maryland

Shreve's sense of place was both his limitation and his strength. Had he been less strongly rooted to place, he might have achieved greater renown as a theorist, but he would not have made the contributions we most value today.

Forrest Shreve was the only child of Henry Shreve and Helen Coates Shreve. Henry Shreve, a Quaker, was born August 3, 1844, in Damascus, Ohio. He later described himself as an inferior student who struggled through grammar school, a contrast to his father, Solomon Shreve, who had earned his diploma from Western Reserve Medical College in Cleveland. Solomon died when Henry was four; his mother, Rachel Coates Shreve, died five years later. The orphaned Henry lived with relatives in Deer Creek, Ohio, until he was apprenticed to a tradesman at the age of eleven or twelve. As an adult, he served as postmaster first in Alliance, Ohio, then in Easton, Maryland, where he and his wife moved shortly after their marriage on December 5, 1868.

Helen Garrison Coates, Forrest Shreve's mother, was born September 12, 1839, into a large, Philadelphia Quaker family. She graduated in 1859 from the Pennsylvania Female College at Perkiomen Bridge. Henry Shreve, in his handwritten memoirs, recalled his reluctance to propose marriage to Helen, his first cousin, partly because of the difference in their ages and partly because he thought "it would be a sacrifice on her part to marry a crippled boy deficient in 'schooling'—[an] uncultured, crude country lad who had grown up in pioneer surroundings." In spite of Henry's initial hesitation, Helen accepted him, and their marriage lasted until her death in 1927.

Forrest Shreve was born in Easton, Maryland, a small town on the eastern shore of Chesapeake Bay, on July 8, 1878. It seems likely that as a child Shreve rambled over the tidal flats and marshes near Easton and collected the wildflowers that grew there. He later attributed his interest in botany primarily to his mother, who emphasized the value of reading and study over that of play or purely physical endeavor, and secondarily to his Quaker upbringing.

Children of Quakers were often encouraged in scientific pursuits, particularly nature study. Quaker tradition taught that the study of nature promoted understanding of God: "the World wearing the Mark of its Maker," as William Penn put it.[7] As an adult, Shreve realized that he was one of many Quaker botanists and horticulturalists since the time of John and William Bartram.[8] Unlike certain other Protestant sects, the Quaker faith seems to place no obstacles between the scientific and the religious outlooks.[9]

Undoubtedly, Shreve's Quaker upbringing helped turn him toward a scientific career and also formed the basis for much of his philosophy and practice. Quakers believe that neither the church nor Scripture alone leads to divine truth; rather, God continually reveals himself and his will to each person through an inner light. Friends espouse equality of the races and sexes, and plain, unostentatious dress. They refuse to support military ventures or other forms of violence. Quakers early developed a reputation for being "stiff as trees"[10]; they would not violate their consciences for the sake of society or government. All this Shreve must have absorbed, for Quaker principles are evident in his dealings with his wife, his colleagues, and his work.

After preparatory education at George School, a Quaker school

Forrest Shreve, about age eight

in Newton, Pennsylvania, and at Easton High School, Forrest Shreve entered Johns Hopkins University in 1898. Founded in 1876, Johns Hopkins was modeled on the German universities of the mid-eighteenth century. The German tradition stressed "pure learning," knowledge for its own sake rather than for utilitarian benefits. At Johns Hopkins this ideal became the concept of pure science, research undertaken without concern for practical application. This bias no doubt strongly influenced Shreve: at an impressionable age he learned that a life of scientific research was the highest goal to which he could aspire.[11]

When Shreve started college, his immediate objective was to become a science teacher. His major subjects were chemistry and biology. Surprisingly, he took only one course in botany as an undergraduate, and that in his third year. His reserved nature, serious demeanor, and lively intellect were evidently well established by his college years, for the caption under his picture in the 1901 yearbook reads, "The world knows nothing of its greatest men." Shreve received his A.B. in 1901, then continued studies towards a Ph.D., which he earned in 1905.

By the time he was a graduate student, Shreve had narrowed his interest to botany. For his dissertation, he studied the developmental anatomy of the pitcher plant, a peat-bog wildflower. Duncan S. Johnson, a highly regarded plant anatomist and morphologist, guided Shreve's research.

A superb teacher, Johnson demanded and received excellent work from his students. Many years later, when Johnson celebrated his thirtieth year in the chair of botany at Johns Hopkins, Shreve told his former professor that "such success as I have been able to achieve has been due to the years of my contact with you." Shreve recalled the many things Johnson taught that were not part of any university curriculum: "how to prepare a paper for publication, how to understand German without translating it, how to raise money without going outside the pale of botany, how to develop plates and print photographs, how to construct a sleeping bag, and how to get wet without grumbling."[12]

Shreve's choice of a career in ecology after studying under an anatomist was not unusual. The first generation of American plant ecologists typically received their degrees in departments of botany and studied under teachers who were primarily, like Johnson, taxonomists, anatomists, or morphologists. In any case, a career in plant anatomy did not appeal to Shreve. Many years later he wrote, "Most purely anatomical work finds me rather cold for I always feel that things of that sort can just as well be done . . . by someone else and that the results are not likely to lead to further investigation, which is always the acid test of a good problem."[13] It seems likely that he found pitcher plant anatomy especially dry compared to the plant's exotic behavior in nature. In fact, his first ecological paper, written while he worked toward his doctorate, was a popular article on pitcher plants and other carnivorous plants.

As Shreve explained in "Some Plants Which Entrap Insects," the highly modified leaves of the pitcher plant are urns partly filled with water. Insects are attracted to a pitcher by its rich red color or by the conspicuous veins near its mouth. Once an insect falls into the pitcher, it is unable to escape. After it drowns, its tissues decay into their component chemicals and are absorbed by the plant. This process provides pitcher plants with nitrogen, which is lacking in their peat-bog habitat.

Leaning heavily on the research of Charles Darwin and others, Shreve reviewed other carnivorous plants of the world and described the morphological adaptations that enable them to trap insects. How could such peculiar adaptations arise? he asked. What purpose do they serve? In raising such questions, he may have discovered that his interest in traditional botany was giving way to the exciting new field of plant ecology.

Shreve was among the few American students and professors who embraced the new field with enthusiasm. Most regarded ecology with a suspicion more suited to phrenology, astrology, or mesmerism. The very word *ecology,* coined by the German zoologist Ernst Haeckel in 1866, was so new that, when it was used in an article in *Science* in 1902, a reader wrote to the editor to complain that the word was not in his dictionary.[14] There was not even general agreement on how to spell the word: the British preferred *oecology*, the Americans *ecology*.

In the late nineteenth century, influenced by the work of European plant geographers and ecologists such as Alexander von Humboldt, Eugen Warming, Andreas Franz Wilhelm Schimper, and Oscar Drude, a few American botanists began investigating plants in relation to the environment. Thomas H. Kearney studied the vegetation of the

Dismal Swamp. Roscoe Pound and Frederic Clements examined the wide expanse of prairie in Nebraska. Henry C. Cowles investigated zonation and succession of plants on Lake Michigan sand dunes. Frederick V. Coville worked in the stony desert of Death Valley, Edgar N. Transeau in the wetlands of the Huron River, John W. Harshberger in Pennsylvania, and Conway MacMillan in Minnesota. These scattered scientists had neither a standardized methodology nor a uniform terminology, and there were no clearly acknowledged leaders among them. Some did not even think of themselves as ecologists. But out of these diffuse and ill-focused beginnings grew the field of ecology, the study of organisms in relation to their environment.

Such was the state of ecology in 1904 when Shreve began fieldwork for a botanical survey of Maryland sponsored by the state Weather Service. The book resulting from this project, *The Plant Life of Maryland*, has been characterized as conventional.[15] Certainly it broke no new ecological ground, but several of its topics foreshadowed Shreve's later work.

Getting Experience

Shreve's first effort in plant ecology showed little of the insight that characterized his later contributions. *The Plant Life of Maryland* was essentially a descriptive account of the vegetation of the state with an appended plant list. Shreve and his coauthors, Mintin A. Chrysler, Frederich H. Blodgett, and Fred W. Besley,[1] divided the state into Coastal, Midland, and Mountain zones, then subdivided each zone into several districts. As head of the project, Shreve described the climate, topography, and soils of each zone. Chrysler reported on the vegetation of the Western Shore District of the Coastal Zone, Blodgett on the Upper Midland District of the Midland Zone, and Besley on forest products of Maryland. Shreve wrote the rest of the vegetation descriptions, about half the book.

In discussing Maryland's plant life, Shreve referred to "floristic plant geography" and "ecological plant geography" rather than ecology as such. His idea of floristic plant geography agrees well with modern definitions. He wrote that the floristic plant geographer first lists all species of plants growing in an area, then

> endeavors to show what families and genera of plants are most abundantly represented in species, what are the relationships of the flora to that of

neighboring areas, what are the probable sources and paths of migration of the species which have entered the area from without, and what are the bounds of distribution of the species not found throughout the area.[2]

Shreve listed the plant species limited to each of the three zones and discussed the floristic affinities of certain habitats (for example, dunes, salt marsh, and swamp forest). He speculated on the role of temperature and "local soil conditions" in determining plant distribution and discussed in general terms plant migration into the state from neighboring regions.

According to Shreve's broad definition, the ecological plant geographer functioned as an anatomist, morphologist, physiologist, and ecologist in an attempt to show how the form, structure, and function of plants corresponded to their "physical and organic environment." Questions that the ecological plant geographer should ask included: What life forms are dominant in the region? Which plants grow together? How do plant associations vary from place to place? How does mineralogy or soil texture determine the nature of the vegetation? How do topography, soil moisture, wind, and other factors affect plant distribution?

This series of questions could have served as an outline for an ecology textbook. In the writing of ecology texts, though, Frederic Clements, whose *Research Methods in Ecology* had appeared in 1905, was first in the field.

By the time he wrote *Plant Life of Maryland*, Shreve had probably already read both *Research Methods in Ecology* and its sequel, *Plant Physiology and Ecology*. In these books Clements prescribed a hierarchical system for classification and description of plant communities, starting at the top with the formation—grassland, for instance, or desertscrub—and descending through four levels to the family—a cluster of poppies or a patch of fireweed. Shreve never agreed that Clements's rigid, detailed system was a useful way of looking at plant communities. In *The Plant Life of Maryland* his vegetation descriptions lacked any sort of formal, hierarchical nomenclature. Rather than referring to a Pine-Oak Association or a Maple-Gum Association as Chrysler did, Shreve simply used names suggested by habitat and physiognomy: Clay Upland Swamps, for instance, or Deciduous

Upland Forest. In fact, Shreve rarely used the term *plant associations* in his book; perhaps even then he was wary of its Clementsian connotations.

Through his many publications Clements became the foremost proponent of plant succession. According to him, succession was a gradual and orderly process in which one group of plants replaced another, eventually culminating in the climax community. In view of Shreve's later rejection of the concept of succession when applied to deserts, it is interesting that in *Plant Life of Maryland* he discussed differences between virgin forests and secondary growth in woodlots without once using the term. He recognized that successional processes were at work but evidently did not want to pin that label on them.

All in all, *The Plant Life of Maryland* was the work of a young scientist who had begun to examine critically and reject certain concepts in ecology but who had too little experience to replace discarded ideas with newer ones of his own. His application of the principles of plant ecology to the vegetation of his native state was sound, and the sizable scale of the project was good preparation for later, larger efforts.

In April 1903, while a graduate student, Shreve visited the Cinchona research station in Jamaica. Located at 5,000 feet above sea level on the southern side of the Blue Mountains, Cinchona had been established as an experiment station by the Jamaican government in 1874. The New York Botanical Garden secured the lease of the buildings and grounds in 1903 and turned them into a botanical research station. The facilities included a six-room house, two greenhouses, two laboratories, and three office buildings sometimes used as dormitories. Travelers to Cinchona usually arrived by ship at Kingston, journeyed by carriage to Gordontown, then ascended to Cinchona on horseback via one of two trails.

On his first visit to the island, Shreve was part of a group that included Duncan Johnson, Lucien M. Underwood of Columbia University, and William R. Maxon of the U.S. National Herbarium, distinguished company that speaks highly of Shreve's abilities. The rain-drenched forests, fog-filled ravines, and lichen-shrouded trees could hardly have been more different from the coastal marshes Shreve knew best, and his mind must have whirled with observations, questions, and explanations. The contrast between Maryland and Jamaica no doubt heightened his desire to become a plant ecologist.

In the autumn of 1905 Shreve returned to Jamaica, this time for six months, under a fellowship from Johns Hopkins University and an assistantship from the New York Botanical Garden. When he arrived at Cinchona in mid-October, he possessed little experience in experimental plant ecology, which was in its infancy then, at least in the United States. Shreve's work in Maryland, although sound, had been limited to cataloging plant associations and weather records. Nevertheless, he was determined to prepare a comprehensive treatment of the physiological plant geography—what we would now call physiological ecology—of the higher elevations of Jamaica's Blue Mountains.

Ecologists distinguish among several areas of ecological study. Physiological ecology is the study of how the internal processes of organisms fit them to their environment; community ecology, the investigation of organisms in association with one another; population ecology, the demographic analysis of populations of organisms; and evolutionary ecology, the study of adaptation of organisms through natural selection. In the early part of this century these distinctions had yet to be made on a conscious level, although in practice different ecologists tended to work in one area or another. Clements, for instance, maintained that ecology was identical to physiology, whereas animal ecologist Victor Shelford asserted that ecology was "the science of communities."[3]

It is possible to trace physiological ecology back to the eighteenth century, but for its rise as a self-conscious endeavor we need go back no further than the turn of the century to the plant geographers Eugen Warming and A. F. W. Schimper.[4] In 1898 Schimper stated in *Plant-Geography Upon a Physiological Basis* that "the ecology of plant-distribution will succeed in opening out new paths on condition only that it leans closely on experimental physiology, for it presupposes an accurate knowledge of the conditions of the life of plants which experiment alone can bestow."[5] Shreve applied this experimental approach to Jamaican rain forests.

Like other early American ecologists, Shreve learned his ecology outside the classroom. It seems likely that much of his work in Jamaica was suggested by his readings, particularly *Plant-Geography Upon a Physiological Basis*. Schimper reported results of transpiration measurements in rice; Shreve measured transpiration of selected plants using the same variables. Schimper precisely outlined the kinds of climatic data that should be collected for ecological studies; Shreve collected exactly those data. Schimper discussed the niche of filmy ferns in tropical forests; Shreve examined the anatomy and morphology of Jamaican filmy ferns. Schimper mentioned wettability of rain-forest foliage; Shreve investigated it in detail. Schimper discussed phenology of tropical plants, including flowering, leaf-fall, duration of leaves, and growth; Shreve began a study of these same phenological events. Schimper's influence even extended to Shreve's description of his research as physiological plant geography instead of physiological ecology.

Once Shreve arrived at Cinchona, he undertook several lines of work simultaneously. He gathered old meteorological records for Cinchona and several other locations, then calculated weekly averages for air temperature, soil temperature, humidity, and rainfall. In addition, he collected weather data of his own—including weekly readings of air temperature, soil temperature, light, humidity, rainfall, and percentage of cloudiness and fog—at locations varying in aspect, elevation, and topography. His experimental work involved measuring the transpiration of certain trees and shrubs in the laboratory while simultaneously recording air temperature, humidity, and the evaporative power of the air.

Shreve also explored the island and informally studied its vegetation. He was especially interested in correlating differences in vegetation with such physical factors as topographic location, elevation, humidity, and rainfall. In the Mabess River Valley in the Blue Mountains, about a three-hour horseback ride from Cinchona, Shreve found the lushest vegetation at 3,000 feet above sea level, where, as he said in "A Collecting Trip at Cinchona," temperature and rainfall combined to create a luxuriant tropical forest with a thick carpet of ferns. He noted that many kinds of epiphytes—mosses, ferns, bromeliads, orchids, and others—covered the trees and shrubs and that even on fern fronds there grew an epiphytic layer of liverworts.

Not surprisingly, at the end of his six-month stay Shreve had not completed his course of study. No doubt he was already planning to return to Jamaica as he left for Baltimore in May 1906 to take up teaching duties at the Woman's College, later known as Goucher College. Here, as an assistant professor, he taught elementary botany, plant physiology, and plant morphology from 1906 to 1908.

It was probably in 1904 or 1905, when Shreve taught at the Biological Laboratory in Cold Spring Harbor, Long Island, that he met Daniel Trembly MacDougal, then assistant director of the New York Botanical Garden. A well-established botanist, MacDougal belonged to a scientific jet set. He spent time every year in Tucson, Arizona; New York City; Washington, D.C.; and Carmel, California. When in New York City, he often stayed at the Cosmos Club, one of four clubs to which he belonged. In Carmel he was part of a literary and amateur theatricals group that included the writer Mary Austin. When in the Southwest, he was an avid hunter and outdoorsman, ready for any challenge the desert posed. A genial, sociable man with a keen sense of humor, MacDougal was unfailingly courteous to colleagues and peers but often abrupt with social inferiors. As a highly visible scientist with membership in numerous professional societies, he was in great demand as a speaker on scientific topics.

In keeping with his busy, almost bustling, life, MacDougal was a prolific author. Between 1884 and 1938 he wrote six books and 138 papers, mostly on plant physiology but also on genetics and plant ecology. Among his important contributions to botany were the dendrograph, an instrument for measuring rates of tree growth, and his investigations of tree growth as related to weather cycles. His best-known ecological study was his investigation of plant succession at the Salton Sea in southern California, but without doubt his most important contribution to plant ecology was bringing Forrest Shreve to the Sonoran Desert.

In 1906 MacDougal was appointed director of the recently established Department of Botanical Research of the Carnegie Institution of Washington. This grandly named department consisted of the Desert Laboratory buildings and grounds in Tucson, Arizona, and a small group of investigators, mainly botanists, who studied the adaptations of desert plants to their environment. The laboratory had been founded in 1903 to ascertain "the methods by which plants perform their functions under the extraordinary conditions existing in deserts."[6] This statement proved to be a mandate for a laboratory devoted to ecological research, the first of its kind. The lab was to be instrumental in the emergence of ecology as a distinct field of research.[7]

The Desert Laboratory building stood (as today) about one-third of the way up Tumamoc Hill, then two miles west of Tucson. The grounds included the hill itself, a dark, rocky knoll that rises eight hundred feet above the surrounding plain, and the terrain to its west, some eight hundred acres in all. A one-lane dirt road and a footpath led from the bottom of the hill to the laboratory building. The vegetation of the hill was hardly in pristine condition, having been grazed by cattle and goats for several decades, but the grounds had been fenced in 1907, protecting the native plants from further harm. Palo verde, saguaro, brittlebush, and creosote bush sparsely covered the rocky slopes.

The U-shaped laboratory building had been constructed in 1903 from the dark brown basalt of the hill itself. Tall windows on the north side provided natural light, and the wide, overhanging roof on the south afforded some protection from the midsummer sun. In 1908 all the researchers shared a single building. Besides the large, general laboratory room, other rooms had been outfitted as physiology and chemistry laboratories, a library, a darkroom, and a greenhouse. An adobe building at the base of the hill served as a private office for MacDougal.

During the laboratory's first few years, only one person was employed full time: William A. Cannon first worked on comparative water use by plants and later investigated roots of desert plants. Visiting scientists included Volney M. Spalding, who studied the vegetation of the Tucson area and the physiology of the creosote

The Desert Laboratory in 1911. Arizona Historical Society

bush; Spalding's wife, Effie, who measured water storage and cold sensitivity of the saguaro; Burton E. Livingston, who worked on soil-water relations of desert soils; and Francis E. Lloyd, who studied the anatomy of the ocotillo. MacDougal himself was a visiting investigator at the Desert Laboratory in 1904 and 1905.

Once he was in charge of the Desert Laboratory, MacDougal set about expanding his empire almost immediately. An energetic man, he traveled extensively in the Southwest to study the distribution of desert vegetation. Perhaps wishing to extend his efforts over a wider range of topics but limited by the amount of time at his disposal, he began to look for an assistant to take over certain projects.

In late 1906, while Shreve was at the Woman's College, MacDougal proposed to Robert Woodward, president of the Carnegie Institution, that Shreve be hired to work for the Department of Botanical Research.[8] The institution could support Shreve for a year and a half while he concluded his rain-forest research, MacDougal suggested.

Shreve was enthusiastic when MacDougal outlined this plan to him early in 1907. During his stay in Jamaica, Shreve confessed, he had had "just about enough experience" to discover some interesting problems "and not enough time afterwards to go at them." With surprising self-assurance he added, "If it would be possible for you to appoint me to a research Assistantship for the calendar year of 1908 at $1200 plus the more expensive parts of my laboratory equipment, I should feel sufficiently interested in the Jamaican work to resign my present place, if I found that necessary, although it will be worth $1600 to me next year, with more in sight."[9] By July 1907 MacDougal had "annexed" Shreve, "subject of course, to the action of the board,"[10] and in January 1908 MacDougal informed Shreve that he had been appointed a member of the research staff at a salary of $1,500. They arranged that he would go to Tucson for a year, thence to Jamaica. In June 1908 Forrest Shreve, then twenty-nine years old, was on his way to Tucson.

A Good Fit All Around

Shreve often told his first impression of Tucson: as soon as he climbed down from the train, he stepped right into the spray of a horse-drawn sprinkler that was laying the dust on the town's dirt streets.[1] One can imagine him—a tall, slender man, almost gaunt, with deep-set eyes, an aquiline nose, and a firm jaw—emerging from the train into the desert heat. No doubt he was wearing Eastern-style clothes: wool pants and jacket, a vest, and a long-sleeved shirt. It did not take him long to adapt to the Southwest, though, and in later years he habitually wore a heavy, silver bracelet, a silk bow tie, and a broad-brimmed Stetson. He could have been a native son of the desert.

Tucson in 1908 was no longer the rough, frontier town of legend where "murderers, thieves, cutthroats and gamblers formed the mass of the population,"[2] but a territorial center of thirteen thousand with many of the appurtenances of civilization, including a university, a railroad, gas lights, a small telephone exchange, a city water system, and electric trolleys. Land ownership and city government had largely passed out of the hands of the original Mexican population and into those of the growing number of Anglo-Americans. Still, Tucson looked more like a Mexican town than an American one, and the wide, treeless, unpaved streets; the squat buildings of adobe brick, some stuccoed, some not; the Mexican women swathed in rebozos; and the brilliant June sunshine and seasonal drought must have seemed foreign indeed to one accustomed to the shady neighborhoods of Baltimore and the humid air of the eastern seaboard.

Upon his arrival, Shreve met the Spaldings, who had been living in Tucson since 1905. For nearly thirty years, Volney M. Spalding had been a botany professor at the University of Michigan, where, as a colleague later recalled, his great contribution lay in "giving scientific training to those who would teach natural sciences in the secondary schools, and in insisting that botany is a science of such great usefulness that it should be taught by one who was prepared to do so."[3] While a professor, Spalding met and married Effie Southworth, a student of his and later an instructor at the university.

Spalding first came to the Desert Laboratory as a visiting investigator in 1903. As happened again and again in the lab's thirty-seven-year history, the desert worked its magic. The elderly Spalding was filled with youthful enthusiasm for the desert and the ecological problems it presented, and upon his retirement from Michigan in 1904, he eagerly took up his new work. At first he investigated water relations of the creosote bush and water uptake by the leaves of various desert plants. Eventually, he began what was to be his major work at the Desert Laboratory—a study of desert plant distribution, which included mapping the occurrence of blue palo verde, velvet mesquite, saguaro, and brittlebush on the laboratory grounds.

By June 1907, however, Spalding had become nearly crippled by arthritis. He told MacDougal, "I need hardly say that this work possesses a great fascination for me . . . but in the present state of my health I could not feel sure of making satisfactory progress in it before I should be under the necessity of laying it down." It would be wise, he said, to "bring to Tucson some young man who has the proper training and who has the enthusiasm for the subject that will enable him to pursue it hopefully for a period of years."[4]

Spalding was relieved and pleased to learn that Shreve would be joining him. He told MacDougal, "While the laboratory will be greatly the gainer by the accession, I think that Dr. Shreve is specially to be congratulated on the opportunity to take up such a piece of work with plenty of time to carry it through. I think it is going to be a good fit all around."[5]

And a good fit it was. Shreve's own love affair with the desert began upon his arrival in Tucson and would not end until his death forty-two years later.

Shreve's new position was a plum. It gave him the chance to concentrate on basic research without the distractions of teaching and committee work, and it provided the opportunity to pioneer in a region that was little known biologically. His situation should have been ideal for making novel contributions and earning scientific repute. Inherent in the advantages of his position in Tucson, however, was a powerful disadvantage: isolated from scientific centers in the East and Midwest, he was often unable to make colleagues understand the importance and relevance of his most innovative contributions.

One of Shreve's first duties at the laboratory was reading the twelve atmometers that had been installed on the grounds and in the nearby Santa Catalina Mountains. Atmometers were immensely popular ecological tools for a short period early in the century: one ecologist complained that he "could hardly travel across the country without stumbling over them."[6] The Livingston atmometer—sometimes called an evaporimeter—was a hollow, clay sphere fitted over a glass tube. The tube was inserted through a hole into a cork, which served as a stopper for a jar of water. As moisture evaporated from the surface of the porous clay, additional water was drawn up into the tube from the jar. Regular readings of the water level provided a measurement of the evaporating power of the air. Livingston and Shreve planned to use these data in a study of the relationship between evaporation and vegetation.

Soon after Shreve arrived in Tucson, MacDougal took him to the top of the Santa Catalina Mountains. The ostensible purpose of the trip was twofold: to acquaint Shreve with certain acclimatization experiments and to familiarize him with the location of the atmometers. Secretly, MacDougal also hoped to ignite Shreve's interest in the ecological problems presented by the vegetation of the mountain range.

From 1908 to 1915 Shreve made at least fifteen trips into the Santa Catalina Mountains, and on most of these he visited MacDougal's acclimatization plots and recorded the condition of the transplants. The acclimatization work, started in 1906, was a study of the effects of elevation and climate upon the phenology, growth, and heredity of various plant species. MacDougal hoped that periodic observations would enable him to learn how flower color, time of bloom, root and stem anatomy, and general aspect were affected by climate. More important, as a neo-Lamarckian, he hoped "to obtain evidence as to the inheritance of acquired characters,"[7] that is, to learn whether changes induced by growing a plant at a higher or lower elevation than normal would be transmitted to succeeding generations grown under other conditions. Although MacDougal believed that Shreve was "taking hold of this acclimatization work in a very satisfying manner,"[8] Shreve was in fact not impressed with the scientific possibilities of the study, and a planned joint paper was eventually written by MacDougal alone.

Besides working in the Santa Catalina Mountains, Shreve spent his first year at the Desert Laboratory writing *Plant Life of Maryland* and planning a final trip to Jamaica. In May or June of 1909 he traveled to the East Coast, married Edith Bellamy on June 17, and left with her for Cinchona shortly afterward.

Soon after he had arrived at the Woman's College, Shreve must have met Edith Coffin Bellamy, a physics instructor there. Edith Bellamy was born in Grand Rapids, Michigan, on November 7, 1878, to Alfred David Bellamy, a physician, and Leonora Coffin Bellamy, a teacher. Edith received her A.B. in 1902 at the University of Chicago, where she majored in physics and chemistry. She began work toward a Ph.D. but never completed it.

Edith Bellamy must have had uncommon drive and intelligence. In a time when few women attended college and fewer still studied science, she vigorously pursued a scientific career. From 1904 to 1906 she served as head of the Department of Science at Judson College in Marion, Alabama, then taught physics at the Woman's College from 1906 to 1909. After her marriage to Shreve, she took up research in plant physiology.

Edith Bellamy, about age twenty

Edith shared much of Shreve's fieldwork until the birth of their daughter in 1918. Shreve supported Edith's career, in itself a remarkable fact given cultural expectations that women would be mothers and housewives and nothing else. No doubt Shreve's upbringing helped form his enlightened attitude. Because Quakers believe in equality of the sexes, Shreve would not have felt threatened by Edith's evident intelligence, and because Shreve's mother had been college-educated, he may have deliberately sought a wife whose horizons were as broad as his own.

The Shreves never published a paper together, although each published separately and with others. There is no evidence that Shreve suggested topics of research to Edith, and in fact it was D. T. MacDougal and B. E. Livingston who were her mentors in plant physiology. Edith was very much a scientist in her own right, and she worked independently of her husband. Their marriage did not begin on this equal footing, however; it was evidently an arrangement they reached after trying a more traditional model in Jamaica.

The Limbo of Controversy

The Shreves arrived in Jamaica on July 1, 1909, after a rough sea voyage that, he said, "gave us both a chance to prove what good sailors we are," and just in time for an earthquake that shook their hotel like "a Southern Railway train" but apparently did little damage.[1] Two weeks later they were settled into Cinchona.

Shreve exercised considerable ingenuity in setting up his laboratory. As he wrote to MacDougal, "I have been building a small physiological dark room and a moist chamber, the former lined with taxonomic drying paper, the latter with peat moss. I have made the moist chamber so that I can get my balances inside it and weigh potted plants without taking them out of the saturated air."[2] Even outside the moist chamber the air was often saturated. At times the humidity was so great that mold grew on Shreve's razor. Excess atmospheric moisture created problems with his experiments, and he told MacDougal, "I am now wrestling with a scheme for warming the balances while in place, to keep the infernal moisture from condensing on them."[3]

His first experiments centered on the water relations of eight characteristic rain-forest plants. He determined what he called the "daily march" of water loss under natural conditions and examined the effect of high humidity and darkness on rate of water loss. He also measured the effect of stomatal behavior on transpiration rate and compared rates of transpiration from stomates and cuticle. Finally, he determined the ratio of transpiration to evaporation throughout the day for each of the eight species.

Simultaneously measuring evaporation and transpiration enabled Shreve to compare transpiration in plants from widely separated localities "with a basis of accuracy which removes this subject from the limbo of controversy into which botanical literature has sometimes seen it descend."[4] He concluded that, contrary to the commonly accepted view that desert plants transpired less than plants of wet regions, "it is the transpiration of rain-forest plants which is low, and the transpiration of desert plants which is high, in terms of unit areas."[5] The corollary to this discovery was that transpiration rates are roughly proportional to evaporation rates; thus in the desert, where the evaporating power of the air is high, transpiration is correspondingly high; in rain forest, where constant high humidity keeps evaporation low, transpiration is also low.

Shreve's emphasis on transpiration may seem odd to present-day ecologists, for photosynthesis, not transpiration, has become the primary focus of physiological ecology. When Shreve worked in Jamaica, however, accurate techniques for measuring photosynthesis in the field did not yet exist, whereas those for measuring transpiration were nearly as reliable as modern methods. The turn of the century was a time of active investigation into the movement of water from the soil through plants into the atmosphere, and in concentrating on the transpiration of rain-forest plants, Shreve was working at the cutting edge of physiological ecology. Shreve did not neglect photosynthesis, however. He found that rain-forest plants grew more slowly than plants of the lowland forests, owing to "low rates of transpiration and adverse conditions for photosynthesis, the former being due chiefly to the prevailing high humidities and the latter to the high percentages of cloud and fog."[6]

The relative transpiration rates of desert and rain-forest plants was not the only myth that Shreve discredited during his time in Jamaica.

He critically examined other widely held beliefs and later published his findings in "The Direct Effects of Rainfall on Hygrophilous Vegetation." Since Darwin's time, Shreve pointed out, biologists had eagerly assigned adaptive functions to a variety of morphological traits. For example, it was widely supposed that the elongated leaf tips characteristic of many tropical plants had evolved to shed excess water. In his laboratory Shreve tested this belief by pinning leaves to an upended board, wetting them, and timing evaporation of water from the leaf surface. He performed this experiment with leaves of eleven different species, first with drip-tips intact, then with tips cut off. Most of the blunt-tipped leaves shed water about as quickly as the drip-tipped leaves, and Shreve concluded that "the efficacy of the dripping point as a means of hastening the drying of the general surface of the leaf has been overestimated."[7] In a related set of experiments he demonstrated that hydathodes, microscopic leaf structures that exude excess water, did not appear to be as important in maintaining the water balance of leaves as previous investigators had thought.

Shreve's criticism of what later ecologists have referred to as "the adaptationist programme"[8] was well in advance of his time. Not until the 1970s did a few ecologists attack the widespread attitude that all traits must have adaptive significance. As S. J. Gould and R. C. Lewontin have argued, "one must not confuse the fact that a structure is used in some way . . . with the primary evolutionary reason for its existence and conformation."[9] Likewise Shreve, sixty-five years earlier, determined that, although drip-tips of leaves might in fact shed water, this did not mean they had evolved for that particular purpose.

Shreve's experiments show that by 1909 he was well launched on his career as a scientist. His willingness to question widely held beliefs continued to characterize his research. Undoubtedly, his Quaker upbringing encouraged accurate observation of nature, and it may have prepared him to be "stiff as a tree" in maintaining unorthodox views.

When not at work in the laboratory, Shreve spent his days roaming the Blue Mountains on horseback and on foot. He concluded that the distribution of vegetation was controlled by two major factors. First, the moisture-laden trade winds created a wet slope on the windward side of the island and a corresponding dry slope on the lee side. The northern side was "fog-drenched and constantly humid, with a rainfall of 160 inches."[10] On the south side the precipitation was fifty-five inches less and the percentage of sunshine far higher, a decidedly warmer and less humid climate. Second, the highly dissected topography created local gradients in humidity and wind action that were reflected in the vegetation. He thought that, in general, temperature was not as important in determining the distribution of vegetation as moisture and topography.

Again Shreve collected climatic data from a variety of habitats, using the Livingston atmometer to measure the evaporating power of the air, hygrographs and psychrometers to measure humidity, and thermographs to measure air and soil temperature. Using these climatic profiles, he could compare the different habitats in terms of climate as well as vegetation.

Shreve defined seven different habitats in the Blue Mountains: Windward Ravines, Windward Slopes, Leeward Ravines, Leeward Slopes, The Ridges, The Peaks, and, rather oddly, Epiphytes. The characteristic plant assemblage of each habitat corresponded to a particular microclimate.

In the forests of the Windward Ravines, trees of "stately size" created a "more or less continuous canopy beneath which undertrees and shrubs form thickets varying in density according as the main forest canopy is more or less open." The terrestrial ferns and flowering plants on the forest floor grew most densely where light penetrated the umbrella of shrubs and trees. "Throughout the lower levels of the forest," Shreve wrote, "garlands of golden-brown mosses . . . clothe the larger trunks and hang from every twig in the undergrowth. On leaning trunks and horizontal limbs are crowded colonies of epiphytic ferns, orchids, and other flowering plants."[11] Constant wetness made this luxuriant growth possible. As Shreve noted, "no picture of the Ravine forests is complete which does not portray the floating fog, in which it is enveloped much of the time, and the reeking wetness which keeps its pads of mosses and hepatics always saturated and its foliage continuously wet for days at a time."

He concluded that the "height and constancy of the atmospheric moisture are the most potent factors in determining the character of the vegetation of the ravines, as well as in differentiating them from other habitats."[12]

Shreve described the other habitats using the Windward Ravines as a standard for comparison. On Windward Slopes the stature of the forest was lower than in Windward Ravines and the canopy more open. Hanging mosses were absent, and thicket-forming ferns took the place of tree ferns. Leeward Ravines differed from Windward Ravines in the lack of hanging moss and filmy ferns and the scanter growth of epiphytes. Shreve explained that the contrast in vegetation between Windward and Leeward ravines was due to climate: "The leeward side of the range receives a lighter rainfall, has much less fog, and a reciprocally increased number of hours of sunshine, factors which combine to lower the atmospheric humidity and increase the insolation to a degree . . . that makes the habitat an unfavorable one for very many of the species so common in the Windward Ravines."[13] The forest of the Leeward Slopes departed still more from typical rain forest. Gone was the distinctive layering; instead there was "little distinction between the crowns of the largest trees and the foliage of the smaller trees and shrubs, so that there is frequently a solid mass of foliage from the canopies to the ground."[14]

In these descriptions Shreve treated vegetation as a continuum, an approach that contradicted the Clementsian view of plant associations as discrete, recurring units. Shreve emphasized that in the Blue Mountains the habitats were not discrete but changed gradually from one to the other. Tree ferns, for example, became less common as he climbed from the damp ravines to the drier slopes, then disappeared altogether on the ridges. He had already observed continua in vegetation before, both in Maryland and when he traveled from the East Coast to Tucson in 1908, but these changes had been gradual and scarcely perceptible. On Jamaica the precipitous topography telescoped vegetational changes. As Shreve rode or walked the forest trails, he gained intimate acquaintance with the shifting of species according to topographic location; as he clambered over the steep slopes, he saw for himself how the abundance of certain species increased or diminished.

Shreve integrated his findings on Jamaica in *A Montane Rain-Forest*. He wrote that, in the rain forest, topography and vegetation are intimately connected because topography "is the agency by which the physical conditions are given their local modifications, and these modifications are in turn responsible for the distribution of forest types."[15] He decided that "no one of the forest types . . . may be looked upon as possessing a closer adjustment to its own complex of physical conditions than does any of the others." In other words, no single community could be selected as representing "the so-called 'climax' forest of the Jamaican montane region."[16] Here again Shreve's ideas contradicted the predominant Clementsian view that under a given regional climate a particular group of plants—the climax association—would prevail. Comparing Jamaican rain forest and Arizona desertscrub, Shreve found that the vegetation of both areas boasted a great diversity of life forms, each highly specialized for the conditions at hand. In its own way the montane rain forest was as unfavorable for plants as the desert because the climatic conditions were just as extreme. The high temperatures, low rainfall, and dry air of the desert were matched by the "prolonged occurrence of rain, fog, and high humidity at relatively low temperatures" of the rain forest. In short, "the collective physiological activities of the rain-forest are continuous but slow; those of the arid regions are rapid, but confined to very brief periods."[17]

A Montane Rain-Forest was well received upon its publication in 1914. One reviewer said that Shreve's experimental approach marked a "new era in the investigation of tropical vegetation," and that his work in Jamaica made "notable contributions to our knowledge of rain-forest phenomena."[18] Fifteen years later, investigators in tropical regions were still citing Shreve's Jamaican studies, and his data on transpiration of rain-forest plants are still valuable.

During his third stay on Jamaica, Shreve visited the desert coast on the south side of the island. He was eager to compare it with the inland desert he had recently come to know in Tucson. Eventually, he reported his findings in "The Coastal Deserts of Jamaica." Because the south side of Jamaica lay in the lee of the Blue Mountains, rainfall was light compared to the windward side of the island—only thirty-two inches a year at Kingston according to Shreve—and supported a savanna of coarse grasses and leguminous trees. Within the savanna were areas of desert where sclerophyllous shrubs and cacti grew. Since these desertlike tracts were always associated with limestone outcrops, Shreve concluded that the Jamaican desert was edaphic rather than climatic. The porous limestone did not retain moisture well and so supported only those plants that could tolerate arid conditions. The humidity and evaporative power of the air were not typical of deserts, but were in fact more like that of the Gulf Coast of Louisiana or Texas. This underscored the edaphic nature of the Jamaican desert.

While Shreve worked in the laboratory and in the field, Edith apparently ran their household. Shreve bought a mule for packing their weekly supplies from Kingston to Cinchona, and he reported to MacDougal,

> By the aid of a sinewy mule, three black people and my wife's tactful management, the domestic ills that flesh is heir to have been reduced to a minimum. Some of the commonest sanitary precautions usually observed by civilized people in all climates have been neglected here for a long time. I had to run a young Canal Zone here for several days, with carbolic acid, whitewash, and spade. All is now salubrious, however.[19]

There is no evidence that Edith helped Shreve with his experiments or accompanied him on his trips around the island. Photographs taken in Jamaica show Shreve attired for fieldwork and Edith dressed in floor-length gowns; he cogitates at his desk and she sits stiffly at a table set for tea as a maid stands in the background. Yet back in Tucson, Edith went everywhere with her husband. Perhaps their six months in Jamaica were a watershed in their relationship. In any case, in Arizona's less rigid atmosphere, they created a pattern that was productive for both.

Energy, Push, and Solid Horse Sense

When the Shreves came back from Jamaica early in 1910, they found several changes at the Desert Laboratory. MacDougal, at the invitation of the Carmel Development Corporation, had established a second laboratory in Carmel, California. This facility, known as the Coastal Laboratory, served as the summer headquarters for most of the Desert Laboratory staff for many years, and eventually MacDougal relocated his operations there. In July 1909 Burton Livingston had resigned from the Department of Botanical Research to become professor of plant physiology at Johns Hopkins University, where he spent the next thirty-one years. After Livingston left, MacDougal approached a young plant physiologist, Herman A. Spoehr, about working at the Desert Laboratory for four months out of the year. Spoehr moved to Tucson in October 1910, and by the summer of 1914 a special chemistry laboratory was being built for him. Volney Spalding, incapacitated by arthritis, had moved to a sanitarium in Loma Linda, California, in July 1909.

Spalding's departure left the *Plant World*, a botanical magazine founded in 1897, without an editor. During his time as editor, Spalding had transformed the *Plant World* from a magazine oriented toward high-school botany teachers to a respectable scientific journal. The content of the journal was, unfortunately, superior to its production. When plant ecologist Edgar N. Transeau pointed out that many of his reprints were "so badly smeared with excess ink that the cuts are mere blotches and the printing difficult to decipher,"[1] MacDougal testily responded, "No one is more keenly conscious of the points you mention than myself." He said that when he had taken over the business end of the *Plant World* it had been losing up to four hundred dollars a year, but that through his efforts the journal at last showed "a clean balance sheet." Striking a conciliatory note, he added, "The public including yourself, have been extremely patient with us. . . . Prof. Spalding's editorial work and contributions such as your own are making it widely known and it now looks as if we should soon receive a support that will justify first class methods of manufacture."[2]

Despite MacDougal's show of optimism, all was not in order at the *Plant World*. As Livingston saw the problem, "most things are done two or three times by different people, each one doing enough to finish the particular job if he had it all his own way." The solution, he told MacDougal, was to put Shreve in charge and leave him alone, because Shreve had "energy and push and solid horse sense."[3] MacDougal took Livingston's advice, and Shreve became editor—not a paying position—in the summer of 1910.

The journal's financial difficulties continued for the first year of Shreve's editorship. Livingston estimated that income from the subscription list fell at least two hundred dollars short of actual costs, and he offered one hundred dollars of his own money to the cause.[4] Other botanists contributed, too, becoming members of the Plant World Association. In exchange for their initial investment, they would—they hoped—eventually receive some return from the profits.

By December 1912 Shreve was able to report to MacDougal that the *Plant World* would reach the end of the year without a deficit. "In fact," he added, "we will have paid 13 printers bills . . . during the calendar year, 11 of them to the new printers, will have wiped up all other outstanding indebtedness and will have more money in the bank than we had on Jan. 1 last year."[5]

For the next seven years Shreve shepherded the little journal, feeding it a steady diet of notes, papers, and comments from colleagues and friends and protecting it from predation. The first potential predator, Frederic C. Newcombe, represented the Botanical Society of America, which at that time did not have a journal of its own. Newcombe asked Shreve how the Plant World Association would react to being subsidized by the Botanical Society as its official organ. Shreve confessed to MacDougal that "the lure of being able to 'enlarge' the P. W. doesn't lure me at all. It would have to print all the truck that was handed over by the Soc., and would lose whatever individuality we may be succeeding in giving it." With characteristic irony he added, "You will recognize that my basic motive is a desire not to lose my lucrative job as editor, much as I may endeavor to obscure this point."[6] Always a politician, MacDougal counseled Shreve to make his reply to Newcombe as "noncommittal, polite, deferential and respectful as you please."[7] The Botanical Society failed in its attempt to secure the *Plant World*, and the journal was safe for the time being.[8]

With his Jamaican fieldwork behind him, Shreve concentrated on learning all he could about the desert and its plant life. Even in Jamaica, desert plants had not been far from his mind, and he had written to MacDougal that "half the story of desert vegetation centers around the seed and the seedling." Unable to resist a dig at Clements, he added, "That's the real point of attack in the matter of the 'dynamics of vegetation' of which we read so much and learn so little."[9]

Without realizing it, Shreve had rediscovered plant population ecology, an area of research that had been virtually untouched since Charles Darwin had monitored plant populations some fifty years earlier. Since Darwin's time, most plant ecologists, including Shreve, had been "vegetationalists." Ecological studies had emphasized "correlations between climate and soils on the one hand and comparative physiology on the other."[10] Plant population ecology, however, emphasized the changes that take place in populations over time and the causes of these changes. When the field took on new life in the 1960s and 1970s, Shreve's early contributions were overlooked. Because Shreve worked with desert plants, population ecologists in more humid regions expected to find little of interest in his work. In addition, he often published in the *Plant World*, which had a limited circulation. Most important, Shreve failed to present his findings in fancy dress. Plant population ecology, like other ecological specialties, is rich in jargon; had Shreve packaged his ideas more attractively, they might have found a warmer welcome.

When Shreve began these studies, he had no models to follow. Of necessity he invented methods to suit the plants at hand. His first subject was the saguaro, a columnar cactus that is one of the most conspicuous plants in the desert around Tucson.

Using data from three different sources, Shreve derived a curve showing the growth rate of saguaros on Tumamoc Hill. Information on seedling saguaros came from tiny plants grown from seed, and Effie Spalding provided several years' worth of figures on juvenile saguaros. Shreve estimated growth of mature plants using photographs taken of the same saguaros at different times. With these data in hand, he plotted rate of growth against height. As he explained in "The Rate of Establishment of the Giant Cactus," the resulting growth curve showed that saguaros grew very slowly at first, then more rapidly as they matured.

Next he measured the heights of a number of saguaros on the rocky slope north of the laboratory building and calculated their approximate ages using his growth curve. He estimated that the oldest individuals were as much as 175 years old. By grouping the saguaros into age classes, he was able to determine when various groups had become established. These calculations produced a curve showing that saguaro establishment had declined between 1865 and 1905. Suspecting that his results were skewed by the location of his stand on a north-facing slope, Shreve repeated his measurements and calculations for a saguaro population on a south-facing slope of the Santa Catalina Mountains, where he found a similar decline. He concluded that the saguaro was not maintaining itself in the Tucson area. Explanations would be futile, however, until he learned more about germination, seedling behavior, and climate.[11]

About the same time, Shreve began a study of the establishment of little-leaf palo verde, a green-stemmed, drought-deciduous tree common in the desert around Tucson. Again he invented methods appropriate to the plant involved. By counting annual rings on cut trunks of 22 palo verde trees and measuring the diameter of those same trees, he derived a curve showing the relationship between diameter and age. Using this information, he calculated the ages and approximate dates of establishment of 146 palo verdes on Tumamoc Hill. As he reported in "Establishment Behavior of the Palo Verde," there had been a decline in the rate of establishment since 1860.

Seeds of little-leaf palo verde germinate abundantly after summer rains begin, and in 1910 Shreve took advantage of a bumper crop of seedlings to examine their survival on a plot 640 meters square. After marking every newly emerged seedling with a small, numbered stake, he returned to his plot every two or three weeks and removed stakes from the seedlings that had died. When he summarized his data at the end of the year, he found that the largest number of seedlings had perished in the dry months that followed the summer rainy season. Following the survivors through successive years, he learned that the high mortality of the first year continued for the next two years, then dropped markedly. Mortality in the first three years was often as high as 97 percent. Later he revised this estimate upward. Observing that mature palo verde trees survive periods of drought by shedding twigs, he concluded that "when a Palo Verde seedling becomes large enough to withstand the loss of some of its branches in the most critical portion of the year, its life is safe from all but droughts of the most extreme severity." Once the trees matured, their death rate fell "to an extremely low figure."[12]

Shreve's interest in seeds and seedlings anticipated a much-discussed topic in plant population ecology—the application of G. F. Gause's competitive exclusion principle to plant communities. According to this theory, every species in a community at equilibrium occupies a different ecological niche. Animal ecologists have been able to test the Gausian hypothesis with better success than plant ecologists. In many communities a wide variety of food and habitats is available for coexisting animal species, making it possible for them to roughly apportion these resources. It is less clear how the principle applies to plants, which all require the same "food"—water, light, and mineral nutrients. In 1977, in a widely quoted paper, P. J. Grubb argued that plant niches have "more to do with requirements for regeneration than with partitioning of the habitat."[13] In other words, as Shreve had said sixty-eight years earlier, "half the story of . . . vegetation centers around the seed and the seedling."

Shreve continued to monitor palo verde establishment over the next seven years. He also studied seedling survival of other desert perennials, among them saguaro, barrel cactus, and ocotillo. His summary of this work, "The Establishment of Desert Perennials," compared seedling survival in arid and wet regions. In humid climates, where crowded seedlings competed for light, insufficient light was the principal cause of mortality. In deserts seedlings had both ample space and light. Because germination occurred during the summer rainy season when the soil was warm and moist, physical conditions favored growth—at least for a little while. As the soil dried out, though, conditions quickly became less hospitable, until the only seedlings that survived were those that had "made a strong root development in favorable spots."[14] Shreve concluded that physical, not biological, conditions control plant establishment in the desert.

Studies undertaken since Shreve's time show that he oversimplified the relationship between desert seedlings and their environment. One ecologist has demonstrated that seedlings of creosote bush experience decreased survival in the presence of mature creosote bush plants.[15] Others have discovered that the survival rate of the seedlings increases when they are protected from animal predators.[16] Another study has shown that, in certain habitats, herbivores limit establishment of little-leaf palo verde seedlings.[17] Biotic factors are far more important for seedling survival than Shreve had allowed.

Shreve had long been interested in the physical aspects of the environment that control vegetation. In Arizona his interest was heightened, probably because here physical factors seemed to take precedence over biological ones. During his early years at the Desert Laboratory Shreve investigated several crucial physical properties, including cold-air drainage, rainfall, and soil moisture.

It was probably Shreve's work in the Santa Catalina Mountains that led him to investigate cold-air drainage, the sinking of cold air

Forrest Shreve in the field about 1915

at night from peaks and ridges to valleys and canyon bottoms. He began by collecting nighttime temperature data from four elevations in the Santa Catalina Mountains and from three locations in the Tucson area. In addition, he spent an evening taking comparative readings of the temperature at 5,100 feet on a canyon slope and nearby at 5,000 feet in the canyon bottom.

As he explained in "Cold Air Drainage," he used these data to draw two curves showing the nighttime temperature gradient. One curve was based on ridge temperatures at 2,600, 4,000, 6,000, and 7,000 feet, the other on temperatures in a valley at 2,300 feet and a canyon bottom at 8,000 feet. The curves predicted that at night a valley would be colder than a ridge at the same elevation. As Shreve explained, cold-air drainage reverses the normal temperature pattern expected on mountains. When cold air flows down a canyon at night, the canyon floor will be appreciably colder than a ridge several hundred feet higher. Similarly, a valley at the base of a mountain range may be colder than a ridge thousands of feet higher.

Shreve was especially interested in the ecological implications of this phenomenon. He had noticed that a number of desert plants in the Santa Catalina Mountains penetrated to higher elevations on ridges than in canyon bottoms. Having already decided that some desert species were limited in their upward distribution by cold, he hypothesized that cold-air drainage made canyon bottoms too cold for them. Ridges, being warmer, were more congenial. Because an alternative hypothesis might be that moisture was the limiting factor, he sampled soil moisture near a canyon bottom and on a nearby slope. He found that during the driest months, when inadequate soil moisture would be most severely limiting to plants, there was "no essential difference between the soil moisture of ridges and canyon bottoms."[18] He concluded that temperature, not moisture, limited the upward distribution of desert plants and added that, conversely, soil moisture, not temperature, limited the downward movement of chaparral and forest plants. Shreve was to explore these ideas more fully several years later in *Vegetation of a Desert Mountain Range as Conditioned by Climatic Factors*.

Another physical factor that caught Shreve's attention was rainfall, particularly as it affected soil moisture. He wrote that ecologists customarily explained plant distribution by referring to annual totals of rain, its seasonal distribution, and the correlation of rainfall and evaporation. For certain investigations, however, he thought it "desirable to replace the consideration of rainfall—which is mediate in its relation to plants—by a consideration of soil moisture, which is immediate in this relation."[19]

Shreve began his study of rainfall and soil moisture by summarizing rainfall data from Tumamoc Hill. He found that between 1905 and 1912 the average yearly rainfall was 14.6 inches. Extremes were 11.11 inches in 1906 and 23.32 inches in 1905. Winter rains—December through March—accounted for 30.5 percent of the total annual rainfall, and summer rains—July, August, and September—accounted for 53.7 percent. The average number of rainy days each year was 61.5. Days of heavy rainfall were much less frequent than those of light rainfall.

Next he sampled soil moisture on Tumamoc Hill at three, fifteen, and thirty centimeters below the soil surface. After making weekly measurements from August 1910 to July 1911, he correlated the rainfall pattern with the soil-moisture pattern and summarized his results in "Rainfall as a Determinant of Soil Moisture." He tentatively concluded that rains of less than 0.10 inch had no effect on the moisture of the soil fifteen centimeters below the surface and that "a conservative approximation of the lower limit of significant rainfalls may be placed at 0.15 in."[20]

In his conclusions he carried one step further the idea that soil moisture rather than rainfall is important to plants. If, he said, he were to calculate the ratio of evaporation to rainfall, he would have a criterion of climate that was useful in a general way. But if he determined instead the ratio of evaporation to soil moisture, he would have a criterion that reflected the actual moisture gain and loss plants meet in nature. Shreve was to expand upon this work in later years. In the meantime it served as a useful guide to further understanding the relationship of desert plants to their environment.

About the time that Shreve studied saguaro populations on Tumamoc Hill, he also investigated the relationship between the distribution of the species and its sensitivity to cold. First he summarized winter climatic data from Yuma, Tucson, Phoenix, and Flagstaff for the winter of 1909—1910, which had been unusually cold. (All but Flagstaff were within the range of the saguaro.) He found that the greatest number of consecutive hours of freezing within the saguaro's range occurred in Tucson—nineteen hours with a minimum of 17° F. Next he subjected a number of small, potted saguaro plants to varying degrees and durations of freezing. They could withstand as much as fifteen hours of freezing temperatures, he discovered, but not as much as twenty-nine hours. The experiments simply confirmed "what might be observed in the field at appropriate times," he wrote in "The Influence of Low Temperature on the Distribution of Giant Cactus."[21]

These results bore out his original hypothesis that saguaros were limited in their northward and upward distribution by the number of consecutive hours of freezing. He noted that many other desert species extended about as far up mountain slopes as saguaro, among them catclaw, little-leaf palo verde, blue palo verde, brittlebush, triangle-leaf bursage, and ocotillo. Their failure to move upslope into regions of more favorable soil moisture was due, Shreve said, to winter cold conditions, which were "such that desert species are unable to survive."[22] Once again he pointed out that climatic factors, not competition with better-adapted species, limited plant distribution.[23]

It is not surprising that Shreve placed little credence in competition as an explanation for plant distribution. In Maryland and Jamaica, plants grew so crowded it was obvious that they competed for light, but in the desert around Tucson he could discern no evidence of such a struggle. Instead, palo verde, saguaro, and ocotillo grew far enough apart that he could easily walk between them. Although seedlings suffered from the seasonal droughts, adult plants had adapted to periodic low soil moisture and apparently did not compete with one another for the available supply of water. Where more favorable moisture conditions existed, as at higher elevations on mountain ranges, cold temperatures, not competition, kept desert plants from taking advantage of the greater soil moisture.

Shreve's idea that desert plants interact more with their environment than with each other was an influential one. His inference became an untested assumption, and only in the 1980s have plant ecologists actually demonstrated competition among desert plants: the saguaro that grows through the sheltering branches of a palo verde tree intercepts the tree's water supply and eventually kills the tree; plants of big galleta, a rhizomatous perennial grass of stable dunes, compete for moisture as the soil dries out.[24]

Shreve's steadfast denial of plant competition in the desert may have stemmed in part from his antagonism toward Clements's ideas. Clements stated in 1916 that competition "is a universal characteristic of all plant communities, and is absent only in the initial stages of succession."[25] Furthermore, he wrote, competition "plays a large part in determining the relative number of occupants and invaders in each stage of a sere."[26] Shreve had reached an incompatible conclusion five years earlier: in the desert "the make-up of the vegetation, the relative abundance of the different types or species, and even, to a large extent, the density of the stand itself are products of the conditions which control germination and the activities of the seedling during its first twelve months."[27] In short, Shreve believed that the composition of desert plant communities resulted from the interactions of seedlings with the physical environment. Clements, on the other hand, stressed competitive interactions between plants at all stages of growth.

This divergence of views can be partly explained by Clements's long association with grasslands, where competition seems obvious, and Shreve's intimate knowledge of deserts, where the phenomenon is obscure. Subjective biases may also have played a part. In any case, by choosing physical over biological factors, Shreve further set himself apart from Clements and his ideas, a trend that was to become more marked with the years.

Tumamocville

In the teens and twenties the Desert Laboratory was so like a small village that some of the inhabitants called it Tumamocville. Its population rose every summer with the influx of visiting scientists and their assistants. In May 1913 MacDougal wryly reported, "We are fast becoming the Mecca of North American botany." Among the expected guests that summer were Burton Livingston, a Professor Fitting of Bonn, Frederic and Edith Clements, a Doctor Crocker of Chicago, and Charles Bessey. "We may really get too popular if we are not careful," MacDougal added.[1]

Dozens of researchers could be accommodated in tent houses that measured about twelve feet by fourteen feet; in fact, MacDougal once told Livingston to "bring as many assistants as you like. We can scatter them out over the desert landscape in whatever form of society may be desirable. Will look up Clements to get ideas on such associations."[2] When the visitors left, Tumamocville was quiet indeed. One summer Shreve reported that "the social atmosphere is not thin, it is completely gone."[3]

Much of the time the atmosphere at the Desert Laboratory was lighthearted. MacDougal reported to Livingston that when two visitors, J. A. Harris and his wife, ended their stay, "pretty nearly everybody in Tumamoc congregated at their tent. . . . Tower (who is now here) acted as auctioneer of their camp furnishings: proceeds, amounting to about $25.00 being turned over to the *Plant World* in cash."[4] Frictions arose frequently enough, however, that periods of complete harmony were noteworthy. As Shreve once reported to MacDougal, "a profound atmosphere of peace and concord enshrouds everything in the village of Tumamoc, even including the social relations of the sundry assistants to each other and to everybody else."[5]

Because living and working conditions on Tumamoc Hill were so intimate, MacDougal tried to find congenial personnel. Once he declined to hire a particular assistant for a second summer on account of the man's "unpleasant personal qualities." As MacDougal explained to the president of the University of Arizona, "the members of our little community at the Desert Laboratory are drawn so closely together that personal qualities are very important in a manner which might not be entirely duplicated in your institution."[6]

When Shreve first arrived at the Desert Laboratory, he lived in a boardinghouse in Tucson. Once Edith joined him, though, they wanted more homelike quarters. They lived in Livingston's house for some time, an arrangement that worked well when Livingston and his wife were in Baltimore but that necessitated moving every summer when the Livingstons returned to Tucson. Most of the temporary researchers and assistants lived in tent buildings on the grounds of the laboratory, and for two years the Shreves did, too. Characteristically, they put a good face on things; in August 1912 Shreve told MacDougal, "At present we are so comfortable in the tent house that we don't care much whether we ever have a house to live in or not."[7] Comfortable or not, they were considering buying land near the laboratory and building a house of their own.

Then, one cold night in January 1913 their tent caught fire from a spark from the stove and burned to the ground. The hill's water system was frozen, and the Shreves lost almost all their possessions in twenty minutes. They moved in with the Spoehrs temporarily and in February hired a man to build a house on some land they had bought from MacDougal. By July they had moved in. Shreve told MacDougal that they had "reopened the New Hotel Shreve, still under the old management; hot and cold water (in afternoon and morning, respectively), fire-escape in every room." Though not quite complete, the house was livable; as Shreve said, "by giving most of our time to it we have now reduced the premises to such a condition that there is nothing undone which cannot wait a few months or a couple of years."[8]

During Shreve's first decade at the Desert Laboratory, MacDougal ordered a number of improvements to the buildings and grounds. He had electricity brought from his office at the bottom of the hill up to the laboratory building. In 1913 he had a private telephone system installed. (An earlier, public phone system had been removed in 1910 following a dispute with the Tucson Chamber of Commerce as to who should pay the bill, and it was decades before the laboratory buildings were put on the Tucson phone service.) The private line connected MacDougal's office and the laboratory building with the shop, the Shreves' house, and the MacDougals' house. About this time, too, a series of stop-gap improvements were made to the one-lane dirt road that wound up the hill.

In 1910 MacDougal bought a thirty-horsepower E. M. F. "motor," as he called it, to use for fieldwork. He paid about four hundred dollars to have the car especially outfitted for the field: extra steel straps braced the frame; large steel boxes on the running boards carried scientific apparatus and equipment; and a rack fastened to the rear of the car held baggage. The car came with a detachable rear seat, or tonneau. MacDougal wrote that "[our] field work is done largely by parties of two, and baggage is stowed in the tonneau without detaching it. . . . By detaching the tonneau we could carry baggage and equipment to nearly half a ton. . . . Practices of this kind have enabled us to cover a wide range of territory."[9]

Godfrey Sykes, explorer, geographer, civil engineer, and MacDougal's right-hand man, said that their cross-country driving inevitably took its toll of the vehicle, so that "mere investigative reconnaissance . . . developed into tests of one's ability as an automotive engineer." Sykes always rose to the challenge, however, whether it was the frame, a wheel, an axle, a steering knuckle, or the drive shaft that was broken. He recalled that "first aid had to be administered in the field by means of spare parts, which the intelligent motorist of those days generally carried with him: bolts, nails, mesquite poles and chunks, and of course the indispensable baling-wire."[10]

Throughout the first decade of the twentieth century, car travel in the Southwest remained problematical. Few roads were paved, and every trip began with local inquiries as to their condition. Shreve and MacDougal greeted the opening of new roads with pleasure, MacDougal because he enjoyed traveling in his various machines, Shreve because they provided new places to collect plants.

Like any good field botanist, Shreve collected wherever he traveled. Until 1942, when two cotton breeders published the first manual for identification of Arizona's native plants,[11] Shreve found naming his specimens a challenge and at times a nuisance. E. O. Wooton and Paul C. Standley published a flora for New Mexico in 1915, and although Arizona botanists often used this manual, it was not wholly satisfactory. Shreve and MacDougal relied to some extent on John James Thornber, the botany professor at the University of Arizona, for identification of local plants, but he was not wholly satisfactory, either. As Shreve told MacDougal, "Thornber is working very faithfully this summer on his bulletin of the cacti, and is learning lots of things that he ought to have been able to tell us long ago, or that we ought to have been able to find out for ourselves."[12]

The situation was further confused by fluid nomenclature. In 1914 Shreve warned MacDougal, "Don't ask me the name of any plant that grows in the Catalinas unless you want to see me throw a fit right in the middle of the street." He reminded MacDougal that they used to call the wild potato by its scientific name of *Solanum tuberosum boreale*. However, Shreve continued, Thornber said that Wooton and Standley had given it a new name. Shreve grumbled, "The one they named was formerly called *S. heterodoxum novomexicanum*, and their dub for it now is *Androcera novomexicanum*. I am not at all sure that this is our plant. Furthermore the *last* thing Thornber said about it was that it 'needs a new name.'"[13]

In 1916 Shreve ordered a herbarium case for his pressed plant specimens. He told MacDougal, "It is a very fine piece of furniture and will do much to foster a respect for our collection of desiccated colloidal gels."[14] As much as Shreve collected, he always remained more interested in living plants than in pressed ones. He once characterized Nathaniel Britton and J. N. Rose, the well-known cactus taxonomists, as "crooning over pieces of blossoms or the fragmentary pelts of cacti that were collected 40 years ago, and have no more relation to a real cactus than a piece of shoe string has to a foxtrot."[15]

Although permanently settled in Tucson, Shreve was far from sedentary. In March 1911 he traveled to White Sands in southern New Mexico. The following month he spent three days with a group of Tucson botanists in the Santa Rita Mountains south of Tucson. In 1912 the Shreves spent several months on the East Coast, mainly so that Edith could pursue transpiration studies with Livingston. Shreve traveled around southwestern Arizona in the spring of 1913 with MacDougal and another plant physiologist. In November and December of that year the Shreves went to Atlanta for the meetings of the Botanical Society of America, where Shreve read a paper, "The Role of Winter Temperatures in Determining the Distribution of Plants." (These winter trips to the East Coast became a yearly trek for Shreve until he retired.) In 1914 he visited the Pinaleño Mountains about eighty miles northeast of Tucson, the Dos Cabezas Mountains ninety miles to the east, and the Mojave Desert in southern California.

A good scientist is as economical as a novelist: no observation is ever wasted, no experience ever lost. Nine years after his Mojave Desert trip, Shreve made use of his observations in a paper on the California deserts. The 1914 trip to the Pinaleños proved to be of more immediate benefit, providing a fruitful comparison with the Santa Catalina Mountains. In 1915 Shreve's travels in the Southwest and his early research at the Desert Laboratory came together in a single landmark publication, a Southwest classic—*The Vegetation of a Desert Mountain Range as Conditioned by Climatic Factors*.

The Shifting Panorama

Shreve treasured the memory of his first ascent into the Santa Catalina Mountains. The ten-day trip, which took place in July 1908 just a few weeks after he arrived in Tucson, was "provocative of scores of questions." Later he recalled, "It was taken for granted that I knew how to tighten my own cinches and was accustomed to an entire day in the saddle, both of which happened to be the case." He found the trip from the base to the top of the mountains "impressive and unforgettable." MacDougal led him from the "parched desert" into "grassy parks of oak, juniper, and manzanita," then "through thickets of oak to the pines." The first night they camped "beside a clear stream bordered by deciduous trees, columbine, rudbeckia, fig-wort, and a score of plants belonging to familiar eastern genera." The day had "unrolled a continually shifting panorama of vegetation" in which the slow changes he had "so recently observed between the Atlantic seaboard and Tucson had been reversed and condensed from 1,500 miles to little more than 15 miles."[1] Answering the questions raised by this first trip occupied the next seven years.

The Santa Catalina Mountains rise from an elevation of 3,000 feet

The Desert Laboratory pack train in the Santa Catalina Mountains

on the desert floor to just over 9,100 feet on Mount Lemmon. Until 1920, when a rough dirt road was constructed up the north side, the only access to the mountains was by foot or horseback. The Desert Laboratory staff generally made the ascent in groups of two or three, with an assistant to help with the pack animals and camp chores. Everyone rode a horse or burro, and an equal number of pack animals carried gear.

Fieldwork in the mountains was not without its hazards. Some sections of trail were in such bad condition that riders necessarily walked their mounts. At least once, one of the pack animals fell over a cliff, "going down exactly as if he was a stuffed figure, and not rolling on any particular axis,"[2] as MacDougal noted. Sometimes weather posed problems, especially early in the spring. After a March trip MacDougal told Livingston that "a storm came up lasting all night, dropping 2-1/2 inches of snow and giving us a temperature of 23°." The next morning he attempted to ride to Marshall Gulch but found six inches of snow on the ridge east of Bear Wallow. "Having done 4 miles in 3 hours," he wrote, "I framed a number of excuses similar to those of the arctic explorers and returned to camp."[3]

Camping in Marshall Gulch, Santa Catalina Mountains: left to right, *Forrest Shreve, the laboratory handyman, and Edith Shreve*

Technical problems with instruments cropped up, too. MacDougal noted that "the interminable rain gauge works by fits and starts; sometimes it does not appear to like the taste of water and rejects it, while at other times it has the appearance of being very thirsty, gulping down anything that comes its way."[4] Once, Shreve found that it had rained so much during July and August that the gauges at 7,000, 8,000, and 9,000 feet were full to the brim, which meant that at least twenty-seven inches of rain had fallen, "and no telling how much more."[5] Another time, two years' worth of atmometer readings had to be discarded when Shreve discovered they were not reliable.

From 1908 to 1915 Shreve visited the Santa Catalina Mountains three to nine times each year between April and October. He traveled a regular route, visiting MacDougal's acclimatization stations as well as weather stations he had established himself. On each trip he read the climatic instruments and made notes for MacDougal on the success or failure of the various transplants.

During 1914 Shreve wrote up the results of his studies of the Santa Catalina Mountains, and in March 1915 MacDougal sent the manuscript of *Vegetation of a Desert Mountain Range* to the president of the Carnegie Institution, saying, "This paper embodies Doctor Shreve's arduous work on the desert mountain tops, with a study of the steep gradient by which both meteorological conditions and plant formations pass into the lowland desert conditions."[6] Although MacDougal stated that *Vegetation of a Desert Mountain Range* was a companion piece to *A Montane Rain-Forest*, which the institution had published the year before, a glance at the table of contents of each book shows that the Santa Catalina book was a departure for Shreve. Gone was the emphasis on autecology, and in its place was a new stress on synecology. In *A Montane Rain-Forest* Shreve had studied how transpiration fitted rain-forest plants for their environment; in *Vegetation of a Desert Mountain Range* he investigated the three gradients of topography, climate, and vegetation to see how the topography determined the climate and, through climate, the vegetation.

Shreve's classic study of the vegetation of the Santa Catalina Mountains was an early gradient analysis. Defined by a later ecologist as "the study of relations of populations and communities along environmental gradients,"[7] *gradient analysis* was a term unknown in Shreve's day. Gradients were a familiar concept, though. Shreve referred often to "the normal altitudinal gradient of vegetation" in the mountains, and in a summary of the research he stated, "The principal aim of this work has been to correlate the climatic gradients of the mountain with the vertical differences of the vegetation."[8]

Although Clements had developed and propounded quantitative sampling methods as early as 1905, Shreve did not use plots in the Santa Catalina Mountains. He evidently trusted his eyes to tell him what he needed to know about the composition and structure of the vegetation. Also, since he believed that the vegetational gradient was "chiefly an adjustment of plant to environment and scarcely at all of plant to plant,"[9] he would have seen no need to measure the association of plants with one another. Instead, he emphasized measurement of physical factors. When Robert H. Whittaker and W. A. Niering conducted their own gradient analysis of the mountains in the 1960s, they measured only the vegetation. They were able to take the physical environment for granted because Shreve had already measured gradients of soil moisture, determined the difference in temperature between north- and south-facing slopes, and proved the effectiveness of cold-air drainage in lowering the temperatures of canyon bottoms.

The first third of *Vegetation of a Desert Mountain Range* described the vegetation. Showing his notable reluctance to delimit plant associations, Shreve found only three broad zones of vegetation where Whittaker and Niering later described seven. Shreve referred to his categories—desert, encinal, and forest—as "regions" or "divisions" rather than as Clementsian formations or associations. Within each region he described further subdivisions: lower and upper desert slopes, lower and upper encinal, and pine forest and fir forest. He noted that these divisions were not discrete units and referred to the "inevitable gradations" between them.[10] In fact, he said, it was impossible to climb five hundred feet without noticing a "material change" in the physiognomy of the vegetation.[11]

The desert region, according to Shreve, "comprised all those portions of the Santa Catalina Mountains in which the vegetation is open, low, and diversified in the assemblage of growth-forms, with a predominance of microphyllous trees and shrubs and an abundance of cacti."[12] Desert vegetation extended from the base of the range to 4,000 feet on north-facing slopes, 4,500 feet on south-facing slopes.

"Encinal" was the region of evergreen oaks. The term, suggested by J. W. Harshberger, came from *encino*, the common name of oak in Spanish. The lowest stands of oak were open and orchardlike and grew at about 4,300 feet on north-facing slopes. At the upper limit of encinal—6,200 to 6,400 feet—the oaks grew densely, forming a closed stand.

Encinal gave way to pine forest at about 5,800 to 6,000 feet on north-facing slopes and about 6,000 to 6,400 feet on south-facing slopes. According to Shreve, the transition was striking: the encinal was closed and low in stature, the pine forest open and tall.

As Shreve worked in the Santa Catalina Mountains, he realized that he could no longer use habitat to classify plant communities as he had in Maryland and Jamaica. On the one hand, using habitat as a criterion gave "a greater rigidity and a wider applicability" to the definition of a plant community. On the other hand, "it confuses cause with effect and makes it impossible to investigate the relation of physical conditions to a community defined in that manner without reopening the whole question of the nature and identity of the community." Shreve concluded that "there is much strong logic to support the view that all necessary definitions and classifications of vegetation should be made on the basis of vegetation alone."[13] He retained this view for the rest of his life.

Shreve devoted a substantial portion of *Vegetation of a Desert Mountain Range* to climate, specifically rainfall, soil moisture, evaporation, humidity, air temperature, and soil temperature. The weather data he obtained between 1910 and 1915 still give a valuable picture of the climate of a southwestern mountain range. Shreve himself was not bothered by the short duration of his climatic records; he felt that more could be learned during a single summer of "intensive meteorological studies" than "could be ascertained by an examination of records of rainfall covering a period of a thousand years."[14] His sampling of climatic factors was thorough enough that he felt confident in stating that "it is always possible to find a slope which exhibits the same intensity of a given factor as that which has already been found on an opposed slope, but it is necessary to go up or down the mountain from 500 to 1,500 feet to do so."[15]

The meat of *Vegetation of a Desert Mountain Range* is its final section, where Shreve attempted to correlate vegetation with climate. To do so, he posited a "normal" gradient of vegetation—the successive bands of desert, encinal, and forest. Although people commonly spoke of this gradient as controlled by altitude, he said, it was in fact determined by two sets of factors which themselves changed with altitude: moisture and temperature.

Moisture factors were critical in determining the vertical distribution of plants. Because rainfall was important largely as it affected soil moisture, Shreve used the ratio of evaporation to soil moisture to compare the water relations of plants in desert, encinal, and forest. He discovered that in the arid foresummer, when lack of moisture is most limiting to plants, the ratio in forest was 1:25, in encinal 20:35, and in desert 35:50. Inadequate soil moisture, he concluded, prevented the downward movement of forest plants into encinal and of encinal plants into desert. The influence of temperature factors—including length of the frost period, greatest number of consecutive hours or days of freezing, and the absolute minimum reached—was even more complex. It was clear that many desert plants—and some encinal plants—were limited in their upward distribution by cold.

Certain conditions caused deviations from the normal gradient of vegetation; among them Shreve included slope exposure, surface flow or underflow, and topographic relief, that is, location with respect to ridges, slopes, or canyon bottoms.

The effect of slope exposure on vegetation had been noted by many ecologists throughout the West, Shreve said. Because solar radiation, soil temperature, and soil evaporation differed on north- and south-facing slopes, the vegetation was dissimilar. He pointed out that in the Santa Catalina Mountains these disparities increased at higher elevations.

Shreve characterized the effect of surface flow and underflow on the distribution of vegetation as "bringing components of upland vegetation of each altitude down along the streamways of the altitudes just below. . . . In this manner the Encinal is traversed by bands of Forest, and the Desert slopes are traversed by bands of Encinal."[16] In streambeds the lowest limit of distribution was depressed by one thousand feet for many species and even by two thousand feet for some, reinforcement for Shreve's idea that the lower limits of encinal and forest plants were determined by moisture availability. (Further reinforcement came from the survival of mountain plants under irrigation in the desert, which showed that mountain species could withstand the heat as long as their moisture supply closely resembled montane conditions.)

The role of topographic relief was to carry desert into encinal, and encinal into forest. "Each of the leading types of vegetation in the Santa Catalinas reaches the uppermost limit of its occurrence on ridges and high south-facing slopes," causing "an interdigitation of the vegetistic regions."[17]

During the course of his research, Shreve worked out several important theories about plant distribution. First, the present vertical limit—either upper or lower—of a species is "the average point at which some particular feature of its physiological activities is met by some particular environmental condition that is preventive or unduly inhibitory to it."[18] Second, minor fluctuations in climate, those taking place over a few years, would be reflected in the rarity of species near their vertical limits. Third, a corollary of the second, changes in climate occurring over longer periods, several hundred years or more, would be reflected in slight movements of the vertical limits of species. Although Shreve was at last willing to admit that competition might determine "the surviving individuals of a stand of young trees" or "the composition of a small community of ephemeral or root perennial plants," he continued to maintain that competition is not "responsible for the finding of a plant in one habitat rather than another" nor for "the exclusion of a species from an area in which it might find favorable conditions."[19]

Shreve had approached the idea of vegetation as a continuum in Jamaica. His studies in the Santa Catalina Mountains enabled him to refine and restate this concept:

> It is nowhere possible to pick out a group of plants which may be thought of as associates without being able to find other localities in which the association has been dissolved. Certain plants may be thought of as having closely identical physical requirements because of their associated occurrence in the same spot. Nevertheless, the fact that the vertical ranges and habitat characteristics of these species will reveal more or less pronounced differences goes to show that each of them has survived in a particular section of the climatic gradient. It is true in the Santa Catalina Mountains, as it is true in all other places, that the associated members of a plant community are not able to follow each other to a common geographical and habital limit. The physical requirements of plants are so varied and so elastic that the composition of a series of communities occupying similar habitats in widely separated places shows the constant overlapping of the ranges of individual species which is due to the physiological inequivalence of these species.[20]

Nonetheless, it was not Shreve who received credit for the continuum concept but Henry A. Gleason, a midwestern plant ecologist, who published on the idea two years after Shreve.

During Shreve's lifetime the major botanical journals of the day paid little or no attention to *Vegetation of a Desert Mountain Range*, and his fellow ecologists ignored the potentially revolutionary ideas it contained. Even MacDougal slighted the book. In the year it was published, MacDougal told the president of the Carnegie Institution that "phytogeography is just emerging from the observational-descriptive stage," an advance "made possible by newly developed methods of measurement mostly devised by Professor Clements."[21] Small wonder that Shreve responded drily to MacDougal's raptures over the fifteen-pound manuscript of Clements's *Plant Succession*. When MacDougal assured him that it was "a great book, as you will see when it comes your turn to look at it,"[22] Shreve replied, "I am glad to hear that Clements's publication is in and that it is a large book."[23] Despite the lack of acclaim for his contribution, Shreve did not seek to publicize his work. Unlike Clements, Shreve was neither an astute biopolitician nor a relentless self-promoter.

Point and Counterpoint

In the 1930s the name Frederic E. Clements was almost synonymous with plant ecology. His textbooks were widely used in college classrooms, and his classification system was incorporated into innumerable theses and dissertations. Almost single-handedly, he created the climate of research for plant ecology in the United States between 1905 and 1950.

Frederic Clements entered the University of Nebraska when he was sixteen and the university itself was but five years older. He earned his B.Sc. in 1894, A.M. in 1896, and Ph.D. in 1898. His interests as a student included the taxonomy, morphology, and ecology of flowering plants and fungi; throughout his life he was prone to make grand sweeps across the field of botany, unable or unwilling to narrow his interests. Clements burst into scientific notice in 1905 with the publication of *Research Methods in Ecology*, the first textbook to deal with practical methods for measuring vegetation and environmental variables. After he earned his doctorate, he taught botany first at the University of Nebraska, then at the University of Minnesota, until MacDougal became his enthusiastic supporter.

MacDougal felt that Clements's talents were wasted in teaching.

In 1913 MacDougal arranged an appointment for him as a research associate in the Carnegie Institution.[1] Clements took a six-month leave of absence from his position as head professor of botany at the University of Minnesota, and in August 1913 he and his wife, Edith, took up temporary residence in Tucson. Largely through MacDougal's efforts, Clements secured a full-time position as a researcher with the Carnegie Institution in 1917. For the next eight years the Clementses worked at the Desert Laboratory in the winters and at the Alpine Laboratory on Pike's Peak in the Rocky Mountains in the summers. In 1925 they moved to Santa Barbara, California, where they lived until Clements's retirement from the institution in 1941.

Clements's most influential ideas involved vegetation classification, plant succession, and the climax plant community. At the top of his hierarchical arrangement of plant communities was the *formation*, which in his terms was synonymous with climax: "a formation . . . is the final stage of vegetation development"[2] under a given regional climate. For every regional climate, only one climax formation was possible. It was a natural unit, not an artificial one, according to Clements. He believed firmly that the formation was an organism, as much as a tree or a person, and like any organism, passed through recognizable stages of youth, maturity, and old age. The climax formation itself was "the adult organism," Clements said, a "fully developed community, of which all initial and medial stages are but stages of development."[3]

Associated with Clements's ideas was an entire vocabulary of new terms: consocies, asocies, ecad, ecesis, chresard, clisere, postclisere, halosere, disclimax, postclimax, and so on. It was impossible to comprehend his numerous works without the aid of a glossary.

Historians of science agree that Clements was the predominant plant ecologist of the first half of this century. In an obituary written for the *Journal of Ecology*, British plant ecologist Arthur G. Tansley recognized that Clements's greatest contribution to ecology was not specific theories of succession or plant association but "a general theory which [led] subsequent workers along the most fruitful lines of research" and thus helped to create a "permanent structure of science." Without such a framework, Tansley wrote, "the amassing of detailed knowledge, and even the most brilliant single discoveries, can have no coherent meaning." Although certain of Clements's ideas may have been flawed or unacceptable in their entirety, his name would "never be forgotten."[4] Ronald C. Tobey, science historian and biographer of Clements, said that "Clements became the first philosopher of ecology. His major principles—fantasies, if not dreams to his critics—shaped the conceptual development of American plant ecology."[5]

On the other hand, some historians and ecologists believe that Clements may have retarded the progress of plant ecology. One of their principal complaints was the artificial and arbitrary nature of his system of vegetation classification. Ecologist Frank Egler described Clements as "driven by some demon to set up a meticulously orderly system of nature, as neatly organized and arranged as the components of Dante's Inferno."[6] Egler added that he showed an "extraordinary ability to take an idea, organize it, break it down, classify it to a degree of minutiae that not only leaves nothing for anyone else to do but defeats its very purpose by giving us ultimate particles which are identical with those we already know."[7]

In 1951 ecologist Robert H. Whittaker pointed out that succession in strict Clementsian terms does not exist anywhere: "Succession does not really lead to a regional climax type," he wrote, "it leads to some kind of climax suited to the specific conditions of the site where succession occurs."[8] Carried to their extreme, Clements's ideas lead, as Egler said, to the realization that "the climax *is* vegetation, is all of vegetation, is completely synonymous with 'vegetation.' So why use the word?"[9]

Clements's concept of the plant association was also gradually discredited and transmuted. In the 1980s, ecological dogma states that natural vegetation is a continuum, not a series of discrete associations. Most plant ecologists believe that plant associations, like constellations, are convenient fabrications.

To some extent, Clements's disproportionate influence on plant ecology can be ascribed to his appearance on the scene when there were no established ecologists in America. In ecological terms, he filled a vacant niche and, in doing so, essentially preempted it for forty years. Clements's influence was also due to his assiduous self-promotion. In 1907 he told MacDougal, "I am especially grateful to find you taking up the study of vegetation by means of adequate methods." Clements meant his own methods, of course. He continued,

> While I am not losing any sleep over the matter, I am disappointed that American ecologists are still content to scratch over the surface of the ground. It is amusing to find the English ecologists, in spite of conservatism and the newness of the work, adopting the new methods of studying formations practically in toto, while in this country nearly everyone is still willing to climb a tall hill and guess at what he sees.[10]

As his success grew, so did his arrogance. By 1916 he was saying that his "earlier concept of the formation as a complex organism . . . is not only fully justified, but . . . represents the only complete and adequate view of vegetation."[11]

Clements excelled at packaging his wares, and this, too, accounts in some measure for his success. The new terms he invented were part of the packaging. The writing of books with concepts rather than places as the central theme—plant succession, plant competition, plant indicators—was another part of it.

Although MacDougal consistently supported Clements, Livingston and Shreve did not. Livingston, a writer of clear, precise scientific prose, objected especially to Clements's prolixity. While editor of *Physiological Researches*, Livingston wrote to MacDougal, "I do hope there'll be no more papers of the Clementsian coloration. I don't like the tints at all. And I sweat blood when I read these repeated citations of the 'Research Methods,' that *awful* book. Doesn't the man realize there's nothing to it?"[12] As Livingston understood, one problem with the jargon of Clementsian ecology—as with all jargon—is that it can become a substitute for comprehension.

Shreve objected to Clements's views as much or more on theoretical grounds. He frequently pointed out in papers—always obliquely—where Clements had erred in discussing desert vegetation. A reader who alternately peruses Clements's and Shreve's writings will discover a subtle point and counterpoint and might deduce that Shreve operated only in reaction to Clements. This was undoubtedly not the case. But it is possible that Clements inadvertently compelled Shreve to define his position on competition, vegetation classification, succession, and so forth, particularly in relation to deserts. Shreve never mounted a direct attack on Clementsian ideas, however. He may have felt constrained by MacDougal's friendship with Clements or by the fact that the Carnegie Institution supported them both.

The social relationship between Clements and Shreve was apparently cordial but superficial. The two men had little in common. Shreve enjoyed tequila in moderation and smoked a pipe; Clements neither smoked nor drank, and as one colleague reported, "it gave him real pain to see other people doing so."[13] Shreve was modest, Clements arrogant; Shreve was witty, Clements humorless. Clements was without doubt more ambitious and productive. Both showed a willingness to help younger colleagues, and both were admired by those who knew them well.

Henry A. Gleason's career also serves as a foil for Shreve's. Born in 1882, Gleason earned his B.S. and M.A. at the University of Illinois and his Ph.D. at Columbia University. He taught botany at the University of Illinois from 1906 to 1909 and at the University of Michigan from 1910 to 1919. During these years he undertook ecological studies of local prairies, forests, and sand dunes. In 1919 he accepted a curatorial position at the New York Botanical Garden and turned from ecology to taxonomy.

One observer has written that Gleason's ecological work "began with heresy, continued in rebellion, and ended in triumph."[14] The heresy was Gleason's anti-Clementsian ideas, in particular his insistence that plants grow in slowly changing assemblages, not in discrete, recurring units. As he put it,

> I examined the floodplain forests of the Mississippi over four hundred miles; I examined the beech-maple forest at many stations from Lake Superior almost to the Ohio River. Each of them formed a continuum . . . and in each the unimportant and scarcely appreciable differences from one mile to the next cumulated into profound differences as miles were measured by hundreds.[15]

This idea was, of course, shared by Shreve, who had written in 1915 that it was "nowhere possible to pick out a group of plants which may be thought of as associates without being able to find other localities in which the association has been dissolved."[16]

Gleason has been called "a man of ideas"[17]; principles and concepts interested him as much as plants themselves, and he used mathematical models long before they were widely employed by plant ecologists. Shreve did not share Gleason's regard for quantitative sampling or mathematical manipulation of data. In other ways, the two men had much in common: both made observations and formed hypotheses that contradicted widely held views; both objected vigorously to Clementsian ideas of plant association and succession; both published heretical ideas that were at first ignored or rejected.

Gleason had some difficulty in publishing his unorthodox theories; in one case he resorted to a geographical journal when botanical editors rejected his work. His 1926 paper on the individualistic concept of the plant association aroused enough interest that a half-day session was devoted to it at the 1926 International Botanical Congress, where, as C. H. Muller reported, Gleason's ideas were "rejected and ridiculed." Muller added that it was "extremely unlikely that any professor carried back to his classroom a Gleasonian inspiration from that session."[18]

Although Gleason lived to see his ideas finally accepted, Shreve died before the revival of the individualistic concept. Shreve's development of the idea was ignored by later ecologists, perhaps because he "buried" it in longer works. Whether inadvertently or deliberately, Gleason himself did not cite Shreve's work on the topic. In any case, plant ecologists were not ready for either man's ideas about plant associations, and it was not until the late 1940s that Gleason's "individualistic concept of the plant association" was resurrected and not until the early 1950s that it was supported by a substantial body of evidence.[19] To be fair to Gleason, it is important to point out that Shreve simply stated the concept of individual tolerances and the vegetational continuum; he did not elaborate upon the phenomenon or name it, as Gleason did. Shreve was not a builder of systems.

Clearly, Shreve's personality contributed to his scientific ideas. He once said, "I do not regard heresy as a vice since I am still proud of several of my ancestors who languished in jail or lost their heads for opinions they were not willing to retract."[20] Had he not been a heretic, he might never have seen a disparity between the Clementsian system and nature itself.

For the most part, Shreve's fellow ecologists were so steeped in orthodoxy that they saw only what Clementsian doctrine prescribed. The ability to see a reality that differs from the orthodox view is a primary characteristic of a great scientist. Shreve possessed this ability, but unfortunately for ecology, he lacked the corresponding ability to impress his views upon others. He failed to turn heterodoxy into a new orthodoxy.

Mountain Islands

Shreve's early interest in floristic plant geography continued to flourish. On a trip with J. J. Thornber into the Santa Catalina Mountains, he took along a preliminary plant list for the mountain range. Later Shreve told MacDougal that "Thornber was as much interested in the list as if it had been a brand new thing to him, and seemed to regard it as endowed with an authoritativeness that I should hesitate to claim for it myself, totally overlooking the fact that I had secured almost all the names from him at some time or another."[1] They went through the list as they sat around the campfire in the evenings, and Thornber added as many species as he could.

Shreve was not satisfied with compiling a simple list; he also wanted to examine the phytogeographical relationships of the desert, encinal, and forest floras. Such an examination was impossible with the scant information on hand, however, so on a 1914 trip to the East Coast he visited the Field Museum in Chicago, where he gathered as much information as he could on the wider distribution of the plants that grew in the Santa Catalina Mountains.

In examining the affinities of the flora, Shreve found that ninety percent of the desert species came from the "Arizona-Sonora Desert" or the "Texas-Chihuahua Desert," and only a few from the Mojave or Great Basin deserts. The dominant species of the encinal region ranged far to the south along both sides of the Sierra Madre, but few went farther north than the Mogollon Rim in central Arizona. The forest region possessed "strong floristic affinities both with the Mexican cordillera and with the Rocky Mountains of Colorado and their southern extension in New Mexico."[2] He tentatively concluded that "The floristic relationships of the Desert and Encinal regions are almost wholly with the Mexican deserts and foothills to the south, while those of the Forest region are divided between the Mexican Cordillera and the Rocky Mountains."[3] Nearly fifty years later, when the flora of the Santa Catalina Mountains was better known, ecologists R. H. Whittaker and W. A. Niering elaborated on Shreve's earlier statement but did not alter its substance.

Over the years Shreve had visited several mountain ranges in the vicinity of Tucson, including the Pinaleño, Santa Rita, Dos Cabezas, and Sierrita mountains. Predictably, he was struck by the similarity in their floras, a likeness all the more remarkable because of the expanse of desert or grassland that separated them. He wrote in 1915 that a solution to this mystery would have to await "a closer acquaintance . . . with the actual mechanisms of transport which are effective in the dispersal of the seeds of desert and mountain plants."[4]

He recognized that plant movements during earlier geological eras could explain the similarity of floras on these mountain ranges. In a statement that was a good fifty years ahead of its time, he wrote that climatic fluctuations in recent geological times would have caused upward and downward movement of the encinal and forest belts. "Such movements," he wrote, "would alternately establish and break the connections between the vegetations of the various mountain ranges and elevated plains, thereby permitting the dispersal and subsequent isolation of species which might find no means of movement across the desert valleys under existing conditions."[5]

Shreve was especially intrigued by the differences in the floras of the Pinaleño and Santa Catalina mountains. After his trip to the Pinaleños in September 1914, he drew up a list of high-elevation plants (mostly perennial herbs) found in the Pinaleños but not in the Santa Catalinas. Sixteen of these were subalpine species occurring above 9,000 feet. The Pinaleños are about 1,550 feet higher than the Santa Catalina Mountains, so Shreve inferred that these species depended upon "physical conditions which exist only above the altitude of the highest point in the Santa Catalina range."[6] Another eight species found below 9,000 feet in the Pinaleños but not at all in the Santa Catalina Mountains were less easily accounted for. Shreve sought to explain their absence from an area where conditions appeared favorable.

By 1915 he had decided that the climate, lithology, and physiography of the two mountain ranges were similar enough that their floristic differences could not be assigned to "physical factors."[7] He determined to test this hypothesis by seeing if certain Pinaleño plants could survive in the Santa Catalinas. In 1916 he collected seeds of fourteen species and planted them at "favorable altitudes and favorable habitats" in the Santa Catalinas. He hypothesized that if "any of the species become established it will indicate that their previous absence was due to their immobility."[8]

By 1919 his seed experiment must have failed, for he reversed his earlier conclusion about the movement of woodland and forest vegetation in response to climatic changes and decided that instead "we can not think of the forest flora as having been derived by the retreat up the mountains of a forest which formerly occupied desert valleys."[9] In "A Comparison of the Vegetational Features of Two Desert Mountains Ranges" he wrote, "We are here brought face to face with the entire problem of the manner in which the isolated desert mountains received their population." He admitted that the problem was large and difficult and the evidence extremely meager. Perhaps reluctantly, he concluded, "There seems to be no evidence, however, in favor of such a radical change of climate within the life of these mountains as to have brought about a continuous lowland vegetation like that which is now confined to the mountain summits."[10] Instead, he hypothesized, long-range dispersal had populated the small mountain ranges from the floras of larger ones. The floras of the smaller ranges were impoverished because they presented a small target for propagules.

From ice-age fossils discovered since the mid-1960s, we know that mountains in southeastern Arizona (like those elsewhere in the West) were indeed subjected to a radical change in climate and may well have been connected by continuous woodland instead of desert. Some ranges may have been linked by coniferous forest in areas where valley grasslands now occur. Thus it is probably not necessary to hypothesize that the smaller mountaintops were populated by long-distance dispersal; many plants could, in all likelihood, have migrated from one range to the next via cool, moist habitats—shaded slopes, canyon bottoms, and so forth. Moreover, as the regional climate became warmer and drier, forest and woodland plants did indeed retreat upslope, isolating certain plants on mountaintops, which is where Shreve found them. However, in thinking of mountaintops as potential sources and destinations of propagules, Shreve anticipated by more than forty years a tenet of island biogeography.[11]

While Shreve pursued his studies in the Santa Catalina Mountains, Edith developed a career in plant physiology, a field parallel to but separate from her husband's. Her background in chemistry fitted her for experimental research, and Shreve would have been able to supply whatever informal botanical training she needed.

During 1911 she started an ambitious project—a study of the influence of atmospheric and soil conditions on the transpiration, water content, and anatomical structure of the little-leaf palo verde. She evidently lacked the skills to carry it out and sought help from Burton Livingston. The Shreves went to Baltimore for several months in the first part of 1912 so that Edith could work with him at Johns Hopkins University. After returning to Tucson, Edith completed her palo verde study and eventually published the results in "The Daily March of Transpiration in a Desert Perennial," a paper still cited in ecophysiological literature.

Shreve treated Edith's career as seriously as his own and frequently referred to her research in his papers. They often worked side by side in the laboratory. In 1915 Shreve wrote to MacDougal, "We ate dinner on the hill for four consecutive nights last week and spent two of the nights up there. Mrs. Shreve was trying out the balanced pot method of determining the water movement in her cacti, and I was drawing the vegetational map toward an early finish,—and doing the cooking."[12] Edith had never learned to cook, so on the evenings when Shreve did not fix dinner they ate at Rossi's, a local restaurant. So wrapped up were they in their work they scarcely seemed to notice the war across the sea.

Our Mutual Arbeit

The irruption of World War I in 1914 did not change the daily pace at the Desert Laboratory immediately. At first MacDougal regarded the war in Europe as little more than a personal nuisance. In December 1914 he complained that he had "done nothing from Sept. 1st except re-arrange plans of the Institution which had been upset by the war."[1] When the United States entered the conflict in 1917, though, MacDougal quickly became active in various programs to help the war effort. He was chairman of a state program aimed at enlisting Arizona families in a food-saving campaign, and he was vice-chairman of the Committee on Scientific Research of the Arizona Council of Defense. Shreve was one of fourteen scientists on the committee, which had been established to deal with scientific questions related to the war.

MacDougal urged Shreve to inaugurate "work that would be of national utility."[2] But Shreve was reluctant to be deflected from his basic research. To placate his employer, he told MacDougal that "the local field work we have started is going to lead to some important results" in connection with land-use classification. He hoped this could be considered a problem of "national utility." Perhaps uncomfortable with this specious reasoning, he admitted, "I have so many small irons in the fire that I would like to remove during the next year that I am not sure it would be advisable for me to undertake anything of an extensive character outside of the instrumentation and distributional work I have already been outlining."[3]

In 1917 Shreve registered for the draft, as did Spoehr. In the end, neither man was called up. Shreve was forced to cancel plans he had made in 1916 to travel to Costa Rica with a group of biologists and never did travel to Central America. Overall, the war had little direct impact on the Desert Laboratory. In fact, in 1914 the war was so far away and so lacking in immediacy that MacDougal had no hesitation in making plans for a comprehensive investigation of the Mojave Desert in southeastern California.

As MacDougal envisioned the project, Samuel B. Parish, a California botanist, would compile the flora; Shreve would describe the vegetation; Edward E. Free, a soil scientist, would analyze the soils; and geographer Ellsworth Huntington would study the geology and geomorphology. MacDougal and Shreve made two trips to the Mojave Desert, one in the fall of 1914, another the following spring, and by May 1915 MacDougal optimistically reported, "Parish has his flora nearly completed. Shreve sees his part clearly, and I am beginning to have some glimmerings."[4] Five months later, MacDougal was forced to cancel the project because of financial problems within the Carnegie Institution.

By April 1916 the fiscal crisis was severe enough that Robert Woodward, president of the institution, threatened to cut the budgets of every department by ten percent. It is possible that the cutbacks hit the Department of Botanical Research particularly hard because of acrimony between MacDougal and Woodward. The two men had clashed as early as 1906, when Woodward chided MacDougal first for inflating his budget for the coming year, then for exceeding it the year before. MacDougal defended himself by pointing out that most of his work was carried on in the field; expenses that seemed unreasonable to Woodward were normal and necessary for fieldwork. Nine years later, Woodward told MacDougal, "To a greater extent than in any other department you and Mr. Sykes have manifested a disposition to overreach your opportunities instead of seeking to establish terms of generous reciprocity with the Institution." He compared MacDougal to a "kind of Tammany politician seeking, to use the politician's phrase, to work the Institution for all it is worth."[5]

In January 1915, before the Mojave Desert project collapsed, Irving W. Bailey, a forestry professor at Harvard University and a member of the advisory board to the U.S. Forest Products Laboratory, proposed that Shreve consider a position with the Forest Service. As Shreve explained to MacDougal, the job "would lie at the Forest Products Laboratory at Madison and at the several Forest Experiment Stations." Admitting to "a natural feeling of revulsion at the sound of a government place," Shreve said that nevertheless the scientific possibilities of the job excited him. The research would be nothing less than a "comprehensive attack on the problems of forest ecology." Though it would be a big undertaking, he thought it "would be worth any man's best blood." He warned MacDougal that he had done "considerable preliminary thinking" about the job and decided it was something they should "discuss in all its lights."[6]

If Shreve was indeed offered the job, he eventually turned it down. But he had considered it seriously, showing perhaps that he was ready for a new challenge. His Santa Catalina work was done and the proposed Mojave Desert study was not his project, but MacDougal's. Shreve soon found the challenge he sought in a project that he and Livingston had started years earlier.

The Shreves spent the first four months of 1916 on the East Coast. While Edith worked with Livingston in his plant physiology laboratory, helping him to perfect the cobalt chloride method of measuring leaf transpiration, Shreve gave a series of lectures to Livingston's students and visited J. N. Rose at the Smithsonian Institution. He also stayed with his parents in Easton for several days, long enough, he said, "to get supersaturated with Atlantic moisture, although my chicken-tension and oyster pressure are still low."[7] During this sojourn, Shreve and Livingston renewed work on the evaporation project they had begun eight years before.

In 1908 Livingston had distributed fifty atmometers to an equal number of volunteers, including Forrest Shreve's father. The volunteers read the instruments weekly and sent the results to Shreve, then at the Woman's College. Livingston and Shreve planned to use the data in a joint paper explaining the distribution of vegetation in the United States in relation to climate, particularly evaporation. Livingston had already published two papers on evaporation, but the joint paper with Shreve was to be "more presumptuous." As Livingston told MacDougal in 1908, it "should be a rather large paper, with the requisite maps of vegetation, rainfall, evap. etc."[8] The "rather large paper" evolved into a book that was finally published in 1921 as *The Distribution of Vegetation in the United States as Related to Climatic Conditions*.

This was not the first attempt to explain the distribution of vegetation in the United States according to one climatic factor or another. The biologist C. Hart Merriam had attempted it in 1894, using temperature to delineate life zones, and in 1905 Edgar N. Transeau, a midwestern plant ecologist who taught at Ohio State University, countered with a system of his own.

Merriam based his life-zone system on the belief that "animals and plants are distributed in circumpolar belts or zones, the boundaries of which follow lines of equal temperature rather than parallels of latitude."[9] He delineated six such belts in the western United States: Arctic, Hudsonian, Canadian, Transition, Upper Sonoran, and Lower Sonoran.

Transeau objected that it was scarcely possible to create "a greater mixture of vegetation types, viewed either from a floristic or ecological standpoint," than Merriam had.[10] In devising his own system, Transeau first mapped "natural vegetation centers" in the eastern United States, then sought the "climatic determinants" of each. He concluded that the ratio of rainfall to evaporation correlated best with patterns in vegetation. The ratio worked, he said, because it involved the four climatic factors of greatest importance to plant life: temperature, relative humidity, wind velocity, and rainfall.[11]

Shreve, like Transeau, objected to the jumbling of distinct floras and faunas in Merriam's system. In 1916, on a visit to the Cuyamaca Mountains in southern California, Shreve found it impossible to interpret the vegetation according to Merriam's life zones. He said that "two almost wholly dissimilar assemblages of plant and animal life occupy the eastern and western slopes of these mountains, and the entire complex of physical conditions is very unlike on the two slopes."[12] Moreover, in southern California as a whole, Shreve discerned at least three distinct floristic areas—the coastal lowlands, the Mojave Desert, and the Colorado Desert—where Merriam recognized only the Lower Sonoran zone. As Shreve pointed out, "the fact that these areas possess dissimilar floras is not of so much importance . . . as the fact that their plants exhibit a striking dissimilarity of habit, structure and anatomy, by reason of their adjustment to the three unlike sets of environmental conditions."[13]

Shreve and Livingston considered Transeau's classification system an improvement over Merriam's and an admirable first attempt; however, Transeau had confined his efforts to the eastern United States, and Shreve and Livingston were primarily interested in the arid West. They hoped to devise a more pragmatic system than Merriam's and a more comprehensive one than Transeau's.

The work went rapidly at first. After collecting climatic observations for a year, they summarized their data, and Shreve prepared a vegetation map to accompany it. At this point, in 1909, Livingston had moved to Baltimore, and he and Shreve saw each other only in the summers at the Desert Laboratory. Livingston did not feel handicapped by the distance between them, though, and in May 1910 he told MacDougal that they would soon begin writing "the Shreve-Liv. Arbeit on climatology and plant distrib." In fact, he said, "I do not think it will take us more than this summer to put it into your hands."[14]

They did not put the paper into MacDougal's hands at the end of that summer, however. Four years later Livingston was telling MacDougal, "The drudgery of the climatological study is about over. Shreve promises he will get at his part seriously this fall." Livingston assured MacDougal that they would send him the manuscript "one of these days" and added that the work of redoing the manuscript three times had paid off in the end. He continued, "I get mainly three kinds of letters in the mail, (1) bills, of course, (2) enquiries as to when and where and for godsake how to get spherical cups [atmometers], (3) enquiries as to these blooming climatic maps. I never intended to be an ecologist but I'm afraid that's my category!!"[15]

In a way, Livingston was right. Although he is remembered primarily as a pioneer in plant physiology, plant ecologists claim him, too. D. B. Lawrence, a student of Livingston's and later an editor of *Ecology*, wrote, "Livingston will always occupy an important place in the history of ecology because he played a vital role in directing ecological research toward precise measurement of the natural environment."[16] He was among the first American ecologists to emphasize experimentation in ecology (others were Clements and Shreve) and also one of the first to take physiological methods into the field. Lawrence claimed that Livingston deserved "top credit" for "welding physiology and ecology together."[17]

Livingston was energetic, vigorous, self-confident, productive, impatient. He impressed his personality on his laboratory, and it became the major center for plant physiological research in the United States. Thirty students received doctorates under him, and many went on to make notable contributions to the field. Livingston believed that students learned best in a research setting, and he complained that "the universities are not starting them off right." He told MacDougal, "What the promising chap needs most is to have the doors opened so that he can see the possibilities and there's no better way to do this than to let him in on a more experienced man's problems."[18]

Livingston's influence on his students is unmistakable. Less easy to discern is his influence on Shreve.[19] It seems likely that Livingston sparked Shreve's interest in the relationship between evaporation and plant distribution. During the ten years when Livingston and Shreve plugged away at their "mutual Arbeit," Shreve was also working in the Santa Catalina Mountains, and the two projects must have mingled in his mind, each illuminating the other.

By 1915 it appeared to MacDougal that Livingston and Shreve were "bringing some of their climatological work to completion."[20] As it turned out, though, this was another false hope, and in January 1916 the Shreves went to Baltimore so that the two men could work on the project without interruption. Shreve reported to MacDougal in February that although their work was far from completed "we have nevertheless got matters to the point where we have a very concrete program ahead of us."[21] It went so well that in April, Livingston told MacDougal, "The great book is on its last legs here" and, he added, would be done in about a month or less.[22] Seventeen months later Shreve wrote to MacDougal, "I am now entering the home stretch with the big publication. . . . Just at present I have it in one of the most important stages of extracting general conclusions from all the work that has gone before, and I have myself so well saturated with it again that I can't get my own consent to leave it."[23]

In 1917 they made tangible progress when Shreve's map of vegetation of the United States was published. Although Shreve's experience in the Southwest, particularly Arizona, was extensive (and of course he knew Maryland and the eastern seaboard well), there was much of the country that he had not seen. To prepare the map, therefore, he used photographs, the scientific literature, and maps published by the Forest Service and the Bureau of Plant Industry.

Distinctly avoiding Clements's lead, Shreve did not call the types of vegetation on the new map "formations" or "associations" but simply gave them brief descriptive titles: Southeastern Mesophytic Evergreen Forest, for example, or Western Xerophytic Evergreen Forest.[24] The map itself he titled "Vegetation Areas of the United States." *Area* was a neutral word that would not align him with Clements. In an explanation of the map, Shreve pointed out that he had delineated the various types of vegetation on "criteria which have to do with the relations of the communities to water-supply and water-loss."[25] This physiological classification was largely theoretical; in practice he seems to have relied on physiognomic characters, particularly "the growth-forms involved, the presence of one or many strata of plants, the open or closed conditions, and the degree of simplicity or complexity of the specific content."[26]

In view of Shreve's later work, the most interesting thing about the 1917 map is his treatment of the deserts. He recognized four subdivisions—California Microphyll Desert, Great Basin Microphyll Desert, Arizona Succulent Desert, and Texas Succulent Desert. Forestalling potential complaints that he had treated the deserts in disproportionate detail, Shreve pointed out that these subdivisions were biologically distinct and, furthermore, that they merited "separation in vegetational work as much as do the deciduous and evergreen forests of the eastern United States."[27] Like most biologists, Shreve tended to see more distinguishing details in the areas he knew best: it is axiomatic that taxonomists are "splitters" when dealing with their own groups and "lumpers" when dealing with all others.

Finally, in 1921, thirteen years after Livingston and Shreve had started the project, *The Distribution of Vegetation in the United States as Related to Climatic Conditions* was published by the Carnegie Institution. The authors' stated goal was a far cry from their original one. In 1908 they had started with the trivial, self-evident, and perhaps circular hypothesis that "the amount of water taken up by the air at any given locality during the vegetative season is an infallible index of the character of the vegetation of the encompassing region."[28] In 1921 they were more cautious and stated, "This publication constitutes an attempt to correlate the distribution of the vegetation of the United States with the distribution of some of the climatic conditions that appear to be most important to plants."[29]

In brief, *The Distribution of Vegetation* comprises numerous (not to say innumerable) maps of plant distribution and tables of climatic data accompanied by copious textual explication. First, Livingston and Shreve mapped the distribution of certain common growth forms, such as evergreen broadleaved trees and microphyllous trees. They mapped groups of species as well; one group consisted of fifteen southeastern deciduous trees, for example. In addition, they mapped a few individual species, such as the tulip tree. Finally, they prepared a second, small-scale map of the vegetation of the United States.

In a series of tables Livingston and Shreve presented extremes for thirty-one climatic variables. Of these, they selected seventeen that showed the greatest relevance to patterns in plant distribution. Among them were number of days in the normal frostless season, normal daily mean precipitation, mean total yearly precipitation, and daily mean evaporation. Then they plotted the relevant climatic factors on their various distribution maps to see where correlations could be found.

These maps and tables were an appetizer to the meat of the book, which was to correlate "features of plant distribution with various intensities of the climatic conditions." The authors also hoped to discover the "extreme range of the climatic differences that may be found within the distributional area of each vegetation, each species or each group of species."[30]

The area of greatest interest to Shreve was, of course, the desert. Here they found that temperature regimes varied greatly from place to place and that towns inside and outside the desert had identical temperature regimes. Obviously, temperature alone could not account for the occurrence of desert. Furthermore, neither total yearly precipitation nor evaporation correlated well with the outline of the desert. However, the isoclimatic line where the ratio of precipitation to evaporation equaled 0.20 was roughly similar to the desert boundary, and from this they concluded that "the desert portion of the United States is very closely limited by the line which indicates a ratio of five times as much evaporation as rainfall."[31] Shreve reiterated this conclusion in a paper published in 1940,[32] but he also acknowledged that biological phenomena can rarely be explained by a single determining factor or a single ratio.

The Distribution of Vegetation bears Livingston's imprint more deeply than Shreve's. It was Livingston, after all, who had been working on the relationship between climate (especially evaporation) and vegetation since at least 1906; between 1907 and 1916 he had published ten papers on the topic. These early papers evince Livingston's long-standing interest in the manipulation of climatic data to yield information useful to plant ecologists. He began quite simply in 1908 by comparing summertime evaporation values with the distribution of vegetation in the United States. By 1913 he was seeking to determine the best method to divide the United States into natural climatic regions, and by 1916 he had devised a new method for calculating indices of temperature efficiency. That same year, he published an equation that combined temperature and moisture values into a single climatic index. Livingston's early attempts at correlating vegetation and climate show a proclivity for single-factor ecology and sweeping conclusions. Such flaws lessened noticeably after he enlisted Shreve's cooperation. One can detect Shreve's influence in these words from a 1911 paper of Livingston's: "Our terms are general, our limits merely approximate, and a host of smaller details explainable on the basis of variations in soil, altitude, etc., are here ignored."[33]

Of all Shreve's works, *The Distribution of Vegetation in the United States as Related to Climatic Conditions* has worn the least well. Despite the years of effort Livingston and Shreve invested in compiling weather records, their data did not consistently correlate well with plant distribution, perhaps, as one scientist has suggested, because of "their heavy reliance on averages of monthly temperatures and grouping monthly means together, especially when confined to only one part of the year."[34] Ecologist Frank E. Egler saw a more serious flaw in the book: "mechanism, causationism, and the factoring of the environment," an outlook that was "outmoded in other fields of science" but still showed "few signs of senility among the ecologists."[35]

Ecologists apparently took little notice of the book in the decade after its publication. No review of *Distribution of Vegetation* appeared in *Ecology*, and in the next ten years the articles in that journal cited it only twice. Few climatologists noticed the book either, and the classification did not receive the wide use Livingston and Shreve had hoped for. Readers may have been daunted by the mass of data presented in more than one hundred maps, tables, and figures, and disappointed by the lack of a single, simple system such as Merriam's life-zone classification. And, although Livingston and Shreve felt that their work more accurately reflected the real conditions in nature, their scheme never supplanted Merriam's, perhaps because the U.S. Biological Survey, then under Merriam's direction, early adopted the life-zone system for all its work.

Although *Distribution of Vegetation* received little recognition, Shreve himself was becoming more widely known, and in 1922 he reached his peak of visibility when he was elected president of the Ecological Society of America. This was one of many responsibilities he assumed during the twenties. Like many scientists, he found that extracurricular duties left him less time for research and that the drawbacks of greater exposure counteracted the benefits.

A Place in the Sun

When Forrest Shreve became its president, the Ecological Society of America was seven years old. Shreve, a charter member, was one of twenty-two American ecologists who had met in Philadelphia on December 30, 1914, to discuss the need for a society. Other founding members included Henry C. Cowles, Victor Shelford, Homer L. Shantz, William A. Cannon, Daniel T. MacDougal, and John W. Harshberger. In 1915 charter members elected Shelford the first president, William Morton Wheeler the vice-president, and Shreve the secretary-treasurer.

As an officer of the new society, Shreve tried to recruit members, particularly among scientists on the Pacific Coast. He told MacDougal, "We are anxious to make the objects of the Ecological Society obvious by announcing some of the events that are planned for this year. . . . If we can advertise such a meeting at San Diego it will help to pull in the Pacific Coast men who ought to join, and might help to bring some of the eastern element out to the coast."[1] Two months later he reported that the enrollment had grown to 164 members, representing "all ages, interests, and degrees of intelligence." He noted that "everybody seems very willing to jump in and do something for the general good, so I think the Society ought to be a very useful one if we can train it properly from the start."[2]

He also tried to recruit papers for the annual meeting. As abstracts of papers trickled in, he reported to MacDougal, "In the final performance the zoologists are going to outnumber us. Graves writes me that he has 71 titles for the Zool. Soc. and that there is only one of them that could, by any stretch of the imagination, be placed on a joint session with ecology."[3] Like any new group, the ecologists yearned to establish a separate identity. Shreve particularly wanted it to be understood that ecologists were distinct from plain zoologists.

At first it seemed desirable for the society to form special committees to carry out original research projects and gather data. In 1916 Victor Shelford appointed Shreve, Livingston, MacDougal, and five others to the first of these, a permanent committee on climatology. Their duties were to "confer with the Weather Bureau" and "to have charge of whatever activities the society may engage in along these lines."[4] Shreve and A. E. Cameron, a Canadian scientist, were to be in charge of soil-temperature matters.

Shreve and Cameron's first project was a soil-temperature survey of the United States and Canada; their goal was to publish a map showing isotherms at different depths. They began to gather soil-temperature data from twenty-nine stations across the United States and Canada but ran into many problems. Several temperature stations had to be discontinued when the observers left. In other cases observations could not be made year-round. At some stations soil thermometers rather than thermographs were used, and the data were not comparable. Finally, after ten years, Shreve and Cameron quietly dropped the project. As Shreve explained to a colleague, their interest in the fragmentary data fell so low that they never published any of it.[5]

Shreve continued as secretary-treasurer until 1920. At times he found the position frustrating, as in 1917 when he complained to MacDougal, "Our Symposium is going to be a farce, with three papers, at least two of which will sound just about like any other papers on the program. A Symposium ought to be prayerfully arranged six months in advance."[6] The influenza epidemic and World

War I combined to make it difficult to find a place for the annual meeting in 1918. Shreve told MacDougal, "The trouble with a resort like Atlantic City is that there is nothing but hotel accommodations,—no lanterns, blackboards nor chart hangers. Of course some of the finest purposes of a meeting can be accomplished under those very conditions, and I am sure the Ecologists will be game for it."[7] By 1919 Shreve was tired of these duties and problems—"loaded up with too much of this clerical work,"[8] as MacDougal put it—and glad to turn them over to A. O. Weese, who held the position for the next ten years.

One of the continuing irritations Shreve faced while secretary-treasurer was the lobbying of the members for an Ecological Society journal. Shreve was against such a journal from the start. "Perhaps it would not be such a serious mistake," he told MacDougal in 1916, "but I am out to oppose it as long as possible." He preferred to see the energies and funds of the society devoted to cooperative research projects. Alternatively, society field trips could be "glorified into a real investigation of some one place, extending over several months, with different members taking turns at the wheel, and the society funds helping out." He seemed to feel that almost anything would be better than another "conscription journal."[9]

MacDougal shrewdly realized that at least part of Shreve's resistance arose from the fear that an ecological journal would mean the demise of the *Plant World*. He warned Shreve, "If you can prevent them from establishing a journal it will be a stroke of statesmanship deserving recognition. We are at a disadvantage in such matters, as low minded persons will be prone to think that a competitor to the *Plant World* is not wanted."[10]

Shreve continued to argue against a journal for several years. His only concession was to suggest that the *Plant World* could print all official notices of the Ecological Society and give a certain number of pages each year to society members. In return, the society could guarantee a certain number of new subscribers and pay a nominal charge for the printed pages. Such a scheme would save "the Ecological Society from doing the same old thing" and help "the P.W. to get a place in the sun" without becoming the official organ of the society.[11]

In September 1919 Barrington Moore, then president of the Ecological Society, wrote letters to both MacDougal and Shreve, carefully outlining the need for a journal but not mentioning the *Plant World*. MacDougal temporized, suggesting to Moore that the matter be referred to a committee for consideration. Finally, Shreve acquiesced to the inevitable, and in November 1919 MacDougal told Moore that although the *Plant World* was "coming along very well and serving its general purpose quite as desired," the Plant World Association would be willing to consider a transfer of the journal to the Ecological Society.[12] In December Moore visited the Desert Laboratory to discuss the transfer. MacDougal reported on these delicate negotiations to Livingston: "The stipulations for which I would vote are that the *Plant World* good will, subscription list and subscription obligations, with the money received for the same in 1920, be handed over to the Ecological Society which would agree to publish the journal, preferably as a quarterly, giving reference to the old *Plant World*."[13] The first issue of *Ecology*, dated January 1920, carried the words "Continuing the *Plant World*" on its cover, a tradition that continued until 1954.

Moore, the first editor of *Ecology*, occasionally made use of Shreve's editorial experience on matters as trivial as whether to print text on the backs of plates and as important as whether to accept papers based on material published elsewhere. Shreve also reviewed papers from time to time and helped to choose a new editor when Moore resigned in 1931. Shreve's advice on this occasion was that the new editor not be under forty. "It is the sort of work that spoils the career of the younger man and spoils the good nature of an older one," he warned.[14]

In 1922 Shreve served as president of the Ecological Society, a prestigious position that in the early years of the society was equivalent to the Eminent Ecologist citation established in 1953.[15] Shreve took on other professional obligations, too, probably from a mixed sense of duty and desire. He must have felt isolated in Tucson, especially once Spoehr and MacDougal had moved to Carmel, and serving on committees was a way of both requiting his profession and of connecting with colleagues. In 1926 he served on a committee for review of papers submitted for the annual meeting of the Southwestern Division of the American Association for the Advancement of Science. The following two years he was vice-president of the Southwestern Division, and in 1929 he served as president. In the mid-twenties Shreve helped Victor Shelford edit *The Naturalist's Guide to the Americas*, a book of brief articles on natural areas in North and South America. Shelford assigned more than one hundred scientists to write manuscripts, and Shreve put the articles into a uniform format.

From 1917 through at least 1922 Shreve served on the Board of Control for *Botanical Abstracts*, which had been started several years earlier by the editors of various botanical journals, Shreve among them. Burton Livingston was editor-in-chief of the first volume, which appeared in 1918. Financial problems eventually forced the abstract journal out of business; from its inception it had been "a hand-to-mouth volunteer operation, a labor of love by dedicated persons."[16] (After the last volume was published in 1926, *Botanical Abstracts* and *Abstracts of Bacteriology* merged to become *Biological Abstracts*.)

At the age of forty Shreve took on new family responsibilities with the birth of his daughter, Margaret, in September 1918. Edith remained in the hospital for several weeks, then was bedridden with phlebitis for some time longer. MacDougal sent several copies of a recent issue of *Science* that contained an article by her. Shreve responded, "Mrs. Shreve is very grateful for the copies of *Science*. Seeing one's name in print appears to have great restorative power."[17] After she regained her health, Edith continued her physiological research.

Shreve's administrative duties at the Desert Laboratory increased abruptly in November 1925 when he was designated "Executive Officer in Charge of Operations of the Desert Laboratory at Tucson, Arizona, with the title of Assistant Director of the Laboratory for Plant Physiology." At the same time, Herman Spoehr, who had been working at the Coastal Laboratory in Carmel since 1920, was assigned a similar position there. According to J. C. Merriam, president of the Carnegie Institution, these administrative adjustments were made so that the Desert and Coastal laboratories would conform with other institution research stations. MacDougal, who supervised both

Shreve and Spoehr for the next few years, found that the changes made it possible for him to "concentrate a little bit more" on his own research.[18] Shreve's new duties included preparing a booth for the institution's annual exhibit, writing the annual report for the *Carnegie Yearbook*, and answering the correspondence addressed to the Desert Laboratory from around the world. After two years he also assumed responsibility for preparing the annual budget, which he then submitted to MacDougal for approval.

These growing obligations and responsibilities cut into the time Shreve had available for research. His first decade at the Desert Laboratory had been steadily productive. Between 1910 and 1921 he had written five papers and one book based on his Jamaican work, and nine papers and another book based on his research in the Southwest. After this initial burst of effort he lost momentum. In the following decade he published one book, itself largely the product of his first ten years at the laboratory, and nine major papers. His output decreased when he was in his forties, an age when many scientists are most productive.

By 1918, however, Shreve was apparently eager to try gradient analysis in another mountain range, and he selected one near the coast this time. His major project during his second decade at the Desert Laboratory was a study of vegetation in the Santa Lucia Mountains near Carmel, California.

The Finest Trip

Once Shreve's work in the Santa Catalina Mountains was completed, there was no need for him and Edith to stay in Tucson during the summers, and between 1918 and 1926 they spent most of every summer at the Coastal Laboratory in Carmel. The Desert Laboratory, like Tucson itself, was nearly deserted in the summer; in the days before evaporative cooling, everyone who could afford to leave did so.

The Shreves spent their first full summer in Carmel exploring the mountains along the coast. MacDougal reported to William Cannon that Shreve was "apparently much taken with the problems which he has uncovered."[1] Summer explorations during the next several years eventually furnished material for a series of papers—"The Vegetation of a Coastal Mountain Range," "The Physical Conditions of a Coastal Mountain Range," and "Soil Temperatures in Redwood and Hemlock Forests."

The Santa Lucia Mountains, where Shreve did most of this work, parallel the Pacific Coast south of Monterey for about one hundred miles. Like the other ranges along the California coast, the Santa Lucia Mountains are low, reaching just 5,844 feet. Throughout the range, tawny grasslands abut patches of deep green chaparral, and in canyon bottoms redwood forests cast dense, cool shade even in the summertime. The variety and beauty of the vegetation was just the thing to capture Shreve's interest and set his mind working along familiar lines.

Shreve worked in the Santa Lucia Mountains for seven summers, from 1918 through 1924. He spent the first few years in ecological reconnaissance. By 1920 he had found a suitable location for a series of weather stations, and he began gathering temperature, evaporation, and soil-moisture data.

Shreve found that the dramatic contrast in vegetation from place to place in the mountains—grassland next to chaparral, oak woodland near redwood forest—could be explained, in order of importance, by "topographic site, slope exposure, distance from the sea, and altitude."[2] Each of these variables operated through microclimatic effects. Topographic site determined how much soil moisture would be available to plants—ridges were drier than slopes, and slopes were drier than canyon bottoms. The ratio of evaporation to soil moisture was ten times greater on ridges than in valleys; this change in moisture from one topographic site to another was "the difference between ridge, covered with chaparral, and valley, forested with redwoods."[3] Slope exposure affected the amount of soil moisture available to plants and also determined the air and soil temperature at a given site. Distance from the sea controlled the amount of sunshine, humidity, and wind. Elevation was of minor importance for the vegetation, especially in comparison to the Santa Catalina Mountains, where "a climb of 5,000 feet completely changes the character of the vegetation."[4]

In naming the plant communities of the Santa Lucia Mountains, Shreve once again avoided Clementsian terminology. He referred simply to Hygrophytic Forest, Mesophytic Forest, Chaparral, and Grassland, in keeping with his treatment of the vegetation of the United States, which emphasized physiognomy over floristics and habitat.

Throughout his work in the Santa Lucia Mountains, Shreve compared them to the Santa Catalinas, just as he had compared the Santa Catalina Mountains to the Blue Mountains of Jamaica. He found that the environmental gradients controlling vegetation changed from one location to the next. In the Blue Mountains soil moisture was uniformly high and had little effect on the distribution of vegetation; in the Santa Catalina Mountains, soil moisture fluctuated greatly, and its effect on vegetation was correspondingly great. The importance of elevation in the Santa Catalina range was not repeated in the Santa Lucia Mountains, but the importance of slope exposure was even greater.

As in the Santa Catalina Mountains, Shreve eschewed quadrats and transects. Although he painstakingly measured a variety of physical factors, he disdained comparable measurements of vegetation. Most likely he felt that quadrat sampling was not the appropriate method for achieving his objective. This bias may have arisen in reaction to Clements's advocacy of quantitative sampling. As Shreve wrote some years later,

> The importance attached by many workers to the social features of plant communities is largely subjective and indeed somewhat homocentric. The relation of the desert plant to its physical environment is very real and extremely important and has a far more vital bearing on the interpretation of the vegetation than do its relations to the biotic environment.[5]

During the twenties Shreve turned his attention from mountains back to deserts. In 1914 and 1915 he had made two trips to the Mojave Desert with MacDougal, and in 1916 he had led a desert field trip for the American Association for the Advancement of Science. His first paper on the desert, "Ecological Aspects of the Deserts of California," published in 1925, summarized the observations he had made on these three trips.

Along its western edge the Mojave Desert was rich in species, Shreve wrote. Characteristic plants included the arborescent Joshua tree, big sagebrush, creosote bush, and white bursage, among others. As one approached the Colorado River, species decreased rapidly in number until the vegetation comprised little other than creosote bush and white bursage. Close to the river, the same set of plants occupied nearly every habitat because soil moisture varied little from one topographic situation to another.

Citing rainfall records from six stations across Arizona and southern California, Shreve demonstrated that the proportions of winter and summer rainfall changed from west to east. The Mojave Desert received most of its rainfall in the winter, whereas the desert around Tucson received about half its rainfall in summer and about a third in winter. The lack of rainfall during the months warm enough for plant growth had important consequences for the vegetation of the Mojave Desert, Shreve said. First, it accounted for the paucity of cacti. Since most cacti could not extract water from cold soil, winter rains did not enable them to survive the long, dry summer. Second, it accounted for the great difference in the floras of the Mojave Desert and the desert around Tucson. Since most of the perennial plants around Tucson germinated following summer rains, they could not, Shreve deduced, sprout during the long, rainless summers in the Mojave Desert and thus never became established west of the Colorado River.

Except around the Salton Sea, the vegetation was in "a very static condition." The low number of dominant species, the similarity of soil moisture from one habitat to the next, and the superb adaptation of the dominant plants to the desert environment combined to create a stable cover of vegetation. It made little sense, Shreve thought, to talk about succession where the "initial, sequential, and final stages" of vegetation were all "characterized by the same species and often by the same individuals."[6]

Shreve may have introduced the topic of succession so he could refute Clements's latest ideas on the subject. According to Clements, the vegetation characteristic of rocky desert slopes—saguaro, ocotillo, palo verde, and other species—was a "subclimax."[7] He wrote that "slowly but nevertheless surely" this community would develop into a true climax formation of creosote bush and bursage.[8]

In fact, this successional pattern occurs nowhere in the Southwest. Communities dominated by saguaro, palo verde, and ocotillo occupy different habitats from those dominated by creosote bush and bursage for complex reasons having to do with physical conditions and, perhaps, the competitive abilities of the different species. Instances of plant succession in the desert are known on old fields, ghost-town sites, and debris flows, but the pattern is far different from that proposed by Clements.[9]

Shreve's denial of desert succession may have been largely semantic. He did recognize processes of vegetational change, such as that occurring on active, barren dunes in northwestern Sonora. Once colonization of mobile sand by big galleta grass and white bursage had begun, the dunes became increasingly stable and eventually afforded a foothold for such woody plants as palo verde, mesquite, creosote bush, and Mormon tea. This is certainly succession, although Shreve did not use the term.[10] Evidently the rigid Clementsian definition of succession made it impossible for him to categorize his observations under that rubric. In the 1980s, however, many ecologists consider a variety of vegetational changes, including changes in abundance or species composition, as instances of succession. If Shreve could have used these looser definitions, he might well have been willing to admit the existence of succession in desert environments.

Shreve lived in the Sonoran Desert for fifteen years before making his first extended trip into Mexico. It was not until 1923, when he was forty-five years old, that he traveled with MacDougal to Puerto Libertad, about two hundred miles southwest of Tucson on the Gulf Coast of Sonora.

Travel in Mexico had been impractical for a number of years because of political turmoil. In 1911 a Desert Laboratory trip to Sonora and the Colorado delta was cancelled when revolution broke out. MacDougal told his zoologist friend William T. Hornaday that "the entire frontier is now in a very troubled state; and it will probably be several years before things are as peaceable as at the time of our crossing [in 1907]. I can assure you that the revolution is revolving much more rapidly than is indicated by the news printed in the eastern papers."[11] The border remained unsettled for several years. Outlying areas in Arizona were occasionally raided by Pancho Villa, and in 1916, when a group from the laboratory set out for southwestern Arizona, Shreve advised them not to venture farther than Covered Wells, about seventy miles west of Tucson.[12]

Even after the raids abated, other problems remained. As MacDougal told a newspaper reporter, "there is in general no drinkable water within a hundred miles of the coast, so that it is necessary in going from the interior to the coast to carry a supply for the return trip."[13] Border crossings could be difficult, and MacDougal and Shreve usually tried to get letters of introduction from the Carnegie Institution to present along with their passports and permits for cameras, automobiles, and guns.

The trip that Shreve and MacDougal made to Puerto Libertad was inspired by an expedition of astronomers who had traveled to the coast to watch the solar eclipse. On this earlier trip someone had taken a photograph of a boojum tree, called *cirio* by the Mexicans. The cirio, one of the Sonoran Desert's more improbable-looking plants, tapers like an upended parsnip from a wide base to a narrow tip. The trunks reach heights of fifty feet or more and sometimes bend under their own weight until the tips nearly touch the ground. MacDougal and Shreve were excited by the discovery of the cirio in Sonora, for until that time it had been known only from Baja California. They felt certain that, if the cirio could have migrated across the Gulf of California, other interesting plants might have, too. The two men set out for the coast in November 1923.

The ten-day trip was an eye-opening experience for Shreve. As MacDougal told Nathaniel Britton, "Shreve and I certainly had one of the finest trips of our lives in Sonora and saw far too many things to be described in a letter."[14] They saw far too many things to be described in a paper, too, but nevertheless Shreve quickly set down some of his impressions in "Across the Sonoran Desert." With irrepressible exuberance he described the plants that were new to him—elephant tree, cirio, cardón—not realizing that he had already become accustomed to plants most of his readers would have considered equally bizarre—ocotillo, saguaro, barrel cactus. He was also struck by the occurrence of familiar plants, such as brittlebush, in new habitats. Around Tucson, brittlebush grew only on rocky slopes, but, Shreve noted, north of Altar it grew in nearly pure stands on alluvial plains. The proximity of desert and ocean interested him, too, and he set up rain gauges at Libertad and in a mountain pass eighteen miles inland. At the pass he also set up a maximum-minimum thermometer. Four months later Gilbert Sykes, son of Godfrey Sykes, returned to read the instruments, and Shreve reported in his paper that the coastal zone was nearly frost-free and also extremely arid.

Another trip to Mexico followed one year later. This time Shreve, MacDougal, and Godfrey Sykes met at the Salton Sea, where MacDougal had been working, and traveled from there to Mexicali, thence to the tidal flats at the mouth of the Colorado River, and finally south along the coast to San Felipe in northern Baja California. Before traversing the tidal flats of the Colorado River, they botanized in the Cucopa Mountains, a desert range some twenty miles south of the international boundary.

The desert at the base of the Cucopa Mountains was the most arid Shreve had ever seen. In "The Desert of Northern Baja California" he wrote that there must be few places "in the western hemisphere where the landscape is more completely devoid of plant life than it is throughout the 30 or 40 miles of our journey in which the tidal flat formed the foreground and the barren hills rose abruptly from its inner edge."[15] Vegetation of the area was the result of "the highly intermittent activity of its plants through many centuries of deficient and irregular rainfall."[16]

Shreve had by now seen enough of the southwestern desert to guess that its various sections differed "chiefly in the frequency and length of the periods in which the plants are quiescent."[17] He had not yet come up with an authoritative treatment of the desert, but he had the germ of an idea.

A Wider Outlook

Shreve's appointment in January 1928 as director of the Desert Laboratory signaled the beginning of a new era for him. Since 1926 he had been in charge of the laboratory, as Spoehr had been in charge of the Coastal Laboratory, both under MacDougal's nominal supervision. In 1928 the Coastal, Desert, and Alpine laboratories were reorganized as the Division of Plant Biology. Spoehr, who was forty-two and had thirteen years of experience in the Carnegie Institution, was promoted to chairman of the division. Shreve, forty-six, with nineteen years' experience, was his subordinate.[1] In 1929 Spoehr moved from Carmel to Palo Alto, where a new laboratory had been built at Stanford University.

Shreve, for his part, continued to occupy MacDougal's old office at the bottom of Tumamoc Hill. Here he and his secretary worked on business matters for an hour or two in the morning before he drove up the hill to spend the rest of the day in the laboratory. The office was by then on the Tucson telephone system, but the lab itself still had only a private line. Shreve, who hated to be interrupted by the telephone, had no desire to change this. If something urgent came up, his secretary could call him on the private line.

Forrest Shreve at his desk

Shreve's office at the Desert Laboratory

It is impossible to say how he felt about being passed over for the administrative job. "Spoehr has a beautiful little laboratory there [in Palo Alto] but he is available to too many people and his telephone rings too often,"[2] Shreve told a colleague in 1929. In spite of their mutual love of the desert, Spoehr and Shreve were worlds apart in their interests and in their approaches to science. Basically a laboratory scientist, Spoehr became best known for his work on photosynthesis, particularly the chemistry of carbohydrates. As an administrator, he proved to be dictatorial. He disliked any flouting of the rules or of his authority, and no matter, from high utility bills to pennies charged for mileage, was too small for his critical attention.

The two men clashed early on. Evidently wishing to make his new authority felt, Spoehr challenged certain items on Shreve's 1928 budget, particularly a request for an additional $415 to put Mrs. Keddington, the part-time secretary, on a full-time basis. "The Desert Laboratory is already a little topheavy in the cost of operating the plant in comparison to amounts paid for scientific work," Spoehr stated and added that, if Mrs. Keddington's nonsecretarial duties would contribute to the scientific work done at the laboratory, Shreve could reasonably request the additional money.[3] Shreve, an awkward politician at best, replied, "I am willing to let the matter of the retention of Mrs. Keddington on full time stand on its own merits. It is evidently clear that I would not want her retention to be taken as an indication that office work as such will require her entire time."[4] This small dispute was typical of the problems that clouded Shreve's relationship with Spoehr in the ensuing years.

Aside from administrative irritations, Shreve's course at the Desert Laboratory looked clear early in 1929. Or at least he thought it did. In February he reported to a colleague that the "general attitude of the Administration toward our program and our future seems to be very favorable."[5] At the same time, however, J. C. Merriam, president of the Carnegie Institution, believed that Shreve was not doing "more with the Desert Laboratory administratively than merely to continue what has existed." Merriam felt that Shreve's research proposals were not "scientifically urgent and outstanding." In fact, Shreve was on trial as an administrator; Merriam concluded that if he did not develop "an important constructive program at [the] Desert Laboratory, consideration should be given to a complete revision of the program as to personnel and objectives, such provision to take effect in the budget of 1930."[6]

In 1930, perhaps in response to Merriam's discontent, Shreve organized a small conference about the laboratory. He hoped for guidance on formulating a program that would coordinate his botanical research with current work on soils, physiography, and climatology, subjects outside his area of expertise. Burton Livingston, Harvey M. Hall, Irving W. Bailey, Frederick V. Coville, W. T. Swingle, and Ralph W. Chaney were among the scientists who attended the meeting, which was held in December 1930 at the Carnegie Institution. The conference was no more useful than such meetings usually are—the group approved Shreve's research plan and suggested that he coordinate his investigations with those of the U.S. Department of Agriculture, the University of Arizona, the Boyce Thompson Southwestern Arboretum, the Citrus Experiment Station of the University of California, and Pomona College. W. T. Swingle suggested that an institute for the study of deserts be organized along the lines of existing oceanographic institutes, an idea that apparently stuck in Shreve's mind.

Other outsiders also took an interest in the future of the Desert Laboratory. E. N. Transeau thought that Shreve should prepare vegetation maps of the desert and distribution maps of important plants. He pointed out that there was still no "readable general description of the desert," even though the laboratory had been in existence nearly thirty years. "I am particularly anxious to have the Desert Laboratory do this work," he said, "because if it is left to Clements we shall have a voluminous description of how the Almighty should have made the desert but didn't."[7]

Shreve's thoughtful consideration of these suggestions shows that he took his new duties seriously. Perhaps he believed more firmly in the original mission of the Desert Laboratory than MacDougal ever had. Woodward had exaggerated when he accused MacDougal of being a Tammany politician seeking to use the institution for all it was worth, but there was some truth in the accusation. MacDougal tended to see himself as a superstar and the laboratory as the firmament in which he shone. His early interest in desert ecology proved to be transitory, and after 1917 he devoted most of his efforts to physiological work. Though he eventually published nearly one hundred papers on subjects ranging from genetics to succession, he let pass an unparalleled opportunity to mount a coordinated attack on the problems of the desert. About the best he did along these lines was to allow Shreve to carry out his own projects. When Shreve took charge in 1928, he was prepared for the challenge MacDougal had let slip by.

In 1930 the Shreves moved from their house at the foot of Tumamoc Hill to a quiet neighborhood near downtown Tucson. They hired a housekeeper, whose arrival changed their lives dramatically. Instead of eating almost daily in local restaurants, they ate at home regularly and also entertained out-of-town visitors there.

By this time Tucson's dirt streets had been paved, and cars and trucks had replaced horse-drawn buggies and wagons. Downtown Tucson had become a bustling place that combined aspects of "a crossroads country store, a small college town, and rodeo week around New York's Madison Square Garden."[8] The population had more than doubled since Shreve arrived, and the city itself covered almost twice as much area.

In 1930 Shreve told a colleague, "Tucson is nearer to the Laboratory than it used to be and we now get deliveries of ice, groceries, and laundry and also have an hourly bus service."[9] He hoped these conveniences would help attract visiting investigators. In describing the Desert Laboratory in *The Collecting Net*, a natural history magazine, he emphasized their location in undisturbed desert and their proximity to stores and housing. He wrote, "The equipment includes two stone laboratory buildings with 12 rooms, a small frame laboratory, a shop, a greenhouse, a number of lath and screen shelters, and a 'cave' with nearly constant temperature conditions." Visiting scientists would be welcome to use the laboratory's library, which contained "the principal botanical, physiological, and ecological journals, as well as those of general scientific interest." Also available was "a small collection of texts, handbooks, reference works, floras, and books relating to the desert regions of the world."[10]

Shreve made full use of the facilities and opportunities that were now his to command. As he told one colleague in 1930, "things have been going on rather slowly here for the last three or four years and I am anxious to enlarge our staff and to get a little more motion on the investigations that seem to me to be most vital to our understanding of the desert."[11] He began by hiring Thomas Dwight Mallery, called T. D. or Dwight, in March 1929, Robert R. Humphrey in August 1930, William V. Turnage in 1931, and Arthur L. Hinckley in 1930 or 1931.

T. D. Mallery was a graduate student at the University of Wisconsin, where he worked as a part-time assistant to Benjamin M. Duggar, a plant physiologist and pathologist. Duggar assured Shreve that Mallery "is well-grounded in general botany, has a fine attitude toward the work and toward his associates, and from every standpoint should fit in to your group. . . . He is one of the most likable fellows imaginable, and he will enter cordially into any type of activity."[12] Shreve said that Mallery would be able to make his choice among several research projects and might even want to carry out two projects simultaneously; "this procedure sometimes retards progress," he wrote, "but on the other hand it keeps a man fresher and widens his outlook on both of the problems in hand."[13] Hoping to find a suitable topic for his Ph.D. dissertation in the desert, Mallery took the assistantship that Shreve offered and came to Tucson expecting to stay ten months. He remained for the next ten years.

Robert Humphrey came to the Desert Laboratory from the University of Minnesota, where he had been a student of William S. Cooper. Shreve had heard that Humphrey "knows more ecology than he does physiology, which sounds rather bad,"[14] but Cooper reassured him that Humphrey would work well under Shreve's direction and that it would do the young man good "to be held down to accurate and careful work." Cooper noted that although Humphrey was "perhaps inclined to be a little over confident as to his abilities and knowledge," this was "natural enough in one of his age and at his stage of training. . . . You will be pleased with his personality I am sure, and also with Mrs. Humphrey, who will accompany him to Tucson."[15] Humphrey stayed at the laboratory for thirteen months, showing "a strong and single-minded interest in his work, . . . tremendous physical energy and a vigorous and original mind."[16]

William V. Turnage came to the Desert Laboratory by accident. As he told it, he was visiting relatives near Tucson when a young man drove a Packard into their yard and asked them to recommend an Indian boy to work for him for fifty cents a week plus board. The young man was Mallery, and Turnage recommended himself. It was, after all, the depression, and he had nothing else to do. His job eventually led to his taking classes part-time at the University of Arizona and graduating six years later with a degree in economics. When Turnage left the laboratory in 1939, Shreve told Livingston that the young man had gone far beyond the required duties of an assistant in investigating climatic conditions on Tumamoc Hill and showed "the capacity for making a good researcher."[17]

Arthur Hinckley, who lacked scientific training, worked at the Desert Laboratory as an assistant and caretaker. He eventually became an ad hoc chauffeur for Shreve during his periods of ill health. It seems likely that Hinckley himself had come to Tucson for health reasons. He suffered from tuberculosis and died in 1943 from heart disease.

Another habitué of the laboratory in the thirties was Howard Scott Gentry. He was not an employee of the Carnegie Institution, as were the others, but an independent investigator. In those years Gentry was trying to earn a living by collecting plants in the Río Mayo drainage in southern Sonora, an area that was virtually unknown botanically. He financed each trip by taking subscriptions for his collections from various institutions, mainly the herbaria of major universities and museums. Shreve subscribed to a set of Gentry's specimens and also gave the young man desk space at the laboratory in 1937. Although Gentry's study area was just outside the desert, Shreve found the collections "full of interest" largely because "the Mayo Valley has a greater rainfall than the valleys north of it, and it is the limit of many sub-tropical plants of close relationship to desert species."[18] At Shreve's suggestion, Gentry wrote a book about the vegetation of the Río Mayo drainage.

These assistants gave the Desert Laboratory a distinctive flavor in the early thirties. All remember their time there with fondness and delight; Turnage called them "golden days."[19] Fifty-three years after a brief stay at the laboratory as a visiting investigator, Eric Ashby recalled it as a "very happy place, informal, friendly, relaxed."[20] Every Saturday the crew adjourned to a local Mexican restaurant for a leisurely lunch, which often turned into an informal seminar on some aspect of plant ecology. Visiting scientists gave more formal seminars, and researchers from the Forest Service and the University of Arizona conducted occasional workshops.

Shreve set the tone for the friendly and informal atmosphere. "One never felt that he was working ***under*** Dr. Shreve but ***with*** him," wrote Humphrey.[21] Shreve allowed investigators to keep their own hours, and when summer days became unbearably hot, some worked at night. Typically, Shreve himself worked past the noon hour and after lunch took a sixty-minute siesta.

Shreve's relaxed attitude may have been partly a matter of necessity. Evidently he had never completely recovered from a case of malaria he had contracted in Jamaica, so a deliberate pace of work was essential to his health.[22] Shreve's easy-going approach may also have stemmed from his Quaker background. Quakers believe that any member of the congregation can have insights worth sharing with the others. Authority is not centralized but diffused throughout the congregation. Although this approach to administration would have made Shreve a pleasant supervisor, it might not have impressed his superiors in the Carnegie Institution.

Nor would Shreve's eccentricities of dress have pleased them much. Shreve customarily wore a hairnet, women's pumps, and women's silk stockings. These days some would be quick to label him a homosexual or transvestite, but those who knew Shreve well—Howard Scott Gentry, Marjorie Denney, William McGinnies, and others—state without qualification that there was nothing effeminate about him. Rather, as Tad Nichols put it, "Shreve was an individualist and didn't care what anybody thought as long as he was comfortable." William McGinnies recalled, "We wore long hair in those days, and when you were driving in an open car, your hair blew about," so Shreve used a net to keep his hair out of his face. Marjorie Denney pointed out that Shreve's feet were long and narrow, and since he could not find well-fitting men's boots, he wore women's shoes. She added that Shreve had sensitive skin—perhaps an allergy to wool—and silk stockings ameliorated the effect of unlined wool pants.[23]

A person who had heard only of these notorious oddities of dress and therefore expected Shreve to be a colorful character would have been disappointed. He was anything but flamboyant. His manner and speech were quiet. He was not aggressive, nor was he adept at manipulating others. He had little of the politician in him, much of the maverick, qualities that enhanced his scientific work but may have detracted from his administrative abilities.

A Splendid Field for Work

Shreve hoped to return to the original mission of the Desert Laboratory once he became its director. For him, this meant ascertaining "the methods by which plants perform their functions under the extraordinary conditions existing in deserts," as the founders had stated nearly three decades earlier.[1]

In 1929 he planned to investigate plant- and soil-water relations, changes in vegetation, prolonged soil processes, and physiology of creosote bush. The studies of soil processes and vegetation change had been started by earlier researchers, but the other projects were new ones requiring new personnel. All were to be conducted at the laboratory.

The following year he refined his goals still further. The ultimate objective of research at the Desert Laboratory was, he said, to answer the question, "Through what means is the desert perennial able to exist under conditions which are fatal to plants native in a moist region?"[2] As much as possible Shreve tried to steer visiting scientists into projects that would help answer this question, and he kept his assistants hard at work on the problem, too. T. D. Mallery studied mineral nutrition of creosote bush, took charge of reading the various weather instruments on the hill, and traveled along the Camino del Diablo in southwestern Arizona to read the long-period rain gauges that had been installed by Godfrey Sykes. Robert Humphrey worked at first on determining wilting coefficients of xerophytic and mesophytic plants, then on measuring soil moisture in situ at Tumamoc Hill. Ernest H. Runyon, a graduate student at the University of Chicago who was spending the summer at the laboratory, began a study of creosote bush reproduction.

These projects evince Shreve's continued emphasis on physiological ecology. As he told a correspondent in 1930, "I have a very strong feeling that the most important advances in ecological work are to be made through the use of physiological methods and the study of the behavior of individual species." He had little sympathy with purely descriptive work, he said, although he was willing to concede that "every new region that is opened up to detailed botanical investigation is worthy of descriptive treatment." Nevertheless, he added, it was very easy to push descriptive ecology "beyond the point of adequate returns."[3]

One of Shreve's first projects as director was to map the vegetation on a series of permanent plots established by Spalding in 1906. (These plots, the longest-running in the history of ecological research, are still being monitored by ecologists in the 1980s.)[4] In 1917, after studying establishment of desert perennials, Shreve had written, "The slowness of growth, great longevity, and low rate of establishment among the perennials give the vegetation of the desert an extremely stable character."[5] He revised this opinion somewhat after remapping the permanent plots.

Spalding had originally set up and mapped two kinds of plots on the Desert Laboratory grounds: small quadrats one meter square for following the yearly changes in annual plants, and larger plots one hundred meters square for observing changes in populations of perennials. In 1928 and 1929 Shreve mapped the vegetation on six of the larger plots and reported on the results in "Changes in Desert Vegetation." He noted that the plots had first been mapped before the laboratory grounds were fenced in 1907. Disturbance from grazing had been intense on the three plots just west of Tumamoc Hill but had been inconsequential on the hill itself. Changes in vegetation between 1906 and 1929 would thus reflect "the amount of disturbance that the vegetation had suffered prior to 1906, and the rainfall conditions of the years immediately preceding the mapping."[6] The tally of gains and losses between the first mapping and the second showed interesting demographical patterns. Populations of large perennials—saguaro, palo verde, and mesquite—lost and gained numbers very slowly, "in keeping with their long lives." Populations of small perennials, on the other hand, had "very great losses and gains over a period of 20 years or more, proving them to be very short-lived plants."[7]

Shreve could discern no consistent trend among the six plots; that is, he found "no indication that the vegetation has undergone changes leading toward the gradual replacement of certain species by other ones. In short, there is no evidence of successional change." Throughout the desert Southwest "the species and even the individuals which are the pioneers in the revegetation of cleared areas remain as the final components of the vegetation."[8]

Under Shreve's direction, Hinckley remapped five of the plots in 1936. In "Thirty Years of Change in Desert Vegetation" Shreve noted once again that the populations of larger, longer-lived perennials had changed much more slowly than those of the shorter-lived, smaller perennials. The most striking feature over the thirty years of observation was an increase in the total plant population from 530 to 1,401 individuals. All the plots shared in this increase, which was due to establishment of small shrubs—triangle-leaf bursage, brittlebush, fairy duster, and coldenia. Grasses had increased from "a negligible component of the vegetation" to nearly three percent of the plant cover.[9] The increase in plants had been greater over the past eight years than over the preceding twenty-two years, showing, Shreve thought, the cumulative effect of protection from grazing.

When two plant ecologists mapped the plots again in the late 1970s, they decided that Shreve's conclusion was incorrect. "It now appears," they said, "that the 1936 peaks [in density] were due to increased soil moisture during the previous interval."[10] On the other hand, they confirmed Shreve's earlier conclusion that the changes in vegetation showed no successional trend.

These permanent plots mark one of the few instances when Shreve used quantitative methods to study vegetation. As noted before, his avoidance of plots may have had something to do with Clements's vigorous espousal of them. (Ironically, Spalding may have been inspired by Clements's *Research Methods in Ecology* to establish the plots in the first place.) Later, in his book on the Sonoran Desert, Shreve noted that he had not made any quantitative studies of the vegetation, which might have been a mild dig at Clements. Evidently, Shreve was confident that his eye would tell him all he needed to know about the structure and composition of plant communities. Furthermore, the shapes of desert plants vary so much from species to species that he may have wondered what, if anything, the number of square inches covered by a saguaro or an ocotillo could tell him. Also, he probably felt that the coverage of plants above the ground was only part of the story, for he was fond of quoting a saying of Cannon's that if the desert were turned upside down it would be a jungle.

Another project Shreve started soon after he took charge of the laboratory was a long-term investigation of creosote bush. He selected this species for intensive physiological studies because it was the quintessential desert plant, tolerant of frost, heat, and drought alike, able to survive in the driest, hottest sections of the desert where few other plants could prosper. As he told Bernard Meyer in 1929, "throughout the history of this laboratory there has been much work on succulents and on economic plants and very little on the non-succulent perennials, which are the plants that really meet and solve the problem of desert existence."[11]

Ernest H. Runyon began studies of germination behavior and natural establishment of creosote bush in 1928, and Shreve continued to monitor Runyon's establishment plots at the base of Tumamoc Hill until at least 1938. Shreve and Mallery grew creosote bush in various types of soils to study its tolerance to calcium. When Eric Ashby, of the Imperial College of Science at London, came to work at the Desert Laboratory for two months in 1931, Shreve had him study the stomatal morphology of creosote bush leaves. Under Shreve's direction, Mallery compared water use by creosote bush and cotton with the aim of discovering the mechanism of drought resistance in creosote bush.

Shreve never summarized the results of these various experiments. Runyon published two papers on drought tolerance of creosote bush, Ashby published one on its leaf anatomy, and Mallery published his dissertation on osmotic values of its leaf sap; but outside the pages of the *Carnegie Yearbook*, the results of the work on establishment and natural reproduction never appeared in print, and the original data have long since been discarded or lost.

Another project that never achieved the finality of print was a study of the vegetation of Avra Valley, northwest of Tucson. Shreve started the project in 1918 to determine whether the sharp differences in vegetation in the valley corresponded to differences in soil texture and aeration. The project was an elaborate one. He mapped the vegetation of two hundred square miles within the valley and defined and mapped five physiographic units as well. He made mechanical analyses of soil from each unit. He placed benchmarks in streambeds, on bajadas, and on playas to measure erosion and deposition within the valley. He photographed the vegetation in areas where soil erosion was active. He followed the changes in soil moisture during the arid foresummer and measured rates of evaporation from soils in place. These investigations continued at least through 1928. In the *Carnegie Yearbook* for that year, Shreve summarized the Avra Valley work, but aside from a paper he wrote with Mallery on the relation between caliche and the distribution of desert plants, he did nothing else with the data. In 1937 he was still planning to write up the results.

Shreve had been interested in soil temperature and soil moisture in the desert since 1910, when he had measured the effect of individual rainfall events on soil moisture at Tumamoc Hill. He expanded this work in the twenties and thirties by investigating soil temperature on north- and south-facing slopes, evaporation from soil, vertical movement of water in soil, and effect of rainfall and runoff on recharge of soil moisture. Turnage provided the brawn for much of the soils work, which he later described as "sheer hell." He recalled, "Perhaps the hardest work I did regularly was sampling soil at various depths for moisture content. Our principal such project called for the boring of a hole every two weeks, six feet deep, taking samples at intervals. . . . Occasionally near the end I would strike a stone and have to begin all over again."[12]

At least one ecologist believed that some of this effort was misdirected. Rexford Daubenmire later pointed out that "simple determinations of percent soil moisture in a soil sample are by themselves utterly meaningless, unless related to soil moisture constants of physiologic significance—the wilting percentage and field capacity."[13] Although Shreve could have determined these constants, he did not do so; thus, according to Daubenmire, "the considerable effort expended in the field was completely wasted."

Shreve and Turnage also constructed a device they called a "percolimeter" for measuring runoff in undisturbed desert soil. As Shreve described it, they built the percolimeter by "trenching around the soil and putting in a cement wall." Next they "excavated under it, placing boards one by one under the block of soil." The result was "a body of soil which is completely isolated from the surrounding soil and has had no disturbance whatever."[14] They dug a cellar underneath the percolimeter for access to instruments that recorded runoff.

The purpose of all this work was to better understand the environment in terms of plants. Shreve, immersed to his elbows or perhaps his hips in dirt, was still seeking to describe—as precisely as he could—physical conditions as plants experienced them. How much rainfall was lost through evaporation and runoff? How much moisture was available to shallowly rooted plants, how much to deeply rooted plants? How often and how hard must it rain for the shallow layers of soil to be moistened again? How much hotter was a south-facing slope than a north-facing slope? How much hotter was the soil in the sun than in the shade? And what did it all mean to desert plants, which, rooted in the soil, were unable to move to a more congenial environment?

Shreve planned to hire a plant physiologist and a soil physicist as part of his permanent staff. In 1927 Jesse Doughty, a soil scientist from Berkeley, had spent several months at the Desert Laboratory, discussing possible projects with Shreve. "He is exactly the sort of man that I had hoped to get hold of,"[15] Shreve told MacDougal, conscious of his own lack of training in soil science. But Doughty was only a temporary consultant. During 1930 Shreve wrote many letters to persuade the Carnegie Institution to fund the two positions, then many more to find suitable candidates. He had lined up two men when, at the end of 1930, word came from the institution that neither position could be filled as soon as Shreve had hoped. The stock-market crash in October 1929 had at first had little effect on the institution, but by the end of 1930 the reverberations were being felt in every department.

Ironically, the depression may have saved Shreve's job. Throughout 1929 and 1930 Merriam became increasingly critical of Shreve's leadership. In a memorandum dated August 5, 1930, Merriam wrote that the success of the Desert Laboratory depended "in large measure upon the availability of someone with vision and judgment; who is at the same time able to see the importance of outstanding problems and to furnish the energy and continuing vigorous support that the work needs in order to carry the program through." Merriam doubted whether Shreve had "either the initiative or the continuing faith in his convictions, and the unswerving purpose, required for bringing a really great program to success."[16] The following month Merriam decided that "if the Desert Laboratory is to be a success, some young man must be found who can work along with Shreve and can be expected to furnish the initiative, clear vision, and administrative ability to carry the program out."[17] Because of the depression, however, he was reluctant or unable to make major personnel changes in the Division of Plant Biology, and Shreve was neither discharged nor supplanted.

During 1931 the financial situation of the Carnegie Institution steadily worsened. In August, Spoehr told Shreve that all departments would have to cut their budgets by ten percent. Shreve, who had hoped to increase his budget by fifteen percent, was forced to cancel plans to bring Bernard Meyer to the laboratory to study soil-water relations of creosote bush. At the end of the year Spoehr told Shreve, "President Merriam has just asked that all departments . . . avoid all expenditures which are not absolutely essential." Though the institution had "thus far avoided the necessity for reducing salaries," Spoehr said, "the serious problems . . . inherent in the administration of all invested funds make it essential that we cooperate."[18]

As the depression deepened, the number of scientists who could afford to spend summers at the Desert Laboratory dropped sharply. In the summer of 1928 the five visiting investigators had included Eduard Schratz, whose research on transpiration of desert perennials was funded by the Carnegie Institution, and E. H. Runyon. The following years had been even busier. In 1929 fourteen scientists had worked at the laboratory for periods of three to twelve months, and forty-two had visited the laboratory for one to ten days. Among the researchers had been the German ecologist Heinrich Walter, who worked from October 1929 to April 1930 on determining the osmotic values of characteristic desert plants. In 1931 the outside investigators had included Eric Ashby; Philip Blossom, a graduate student at the University of Michigan, who investigated the habits and local distribution of small rodents in southern Arizona; E. H. Runyon, who continued his studies of creosote bush; E. J. Kraus, of the University of Chicago; and Earl Working, of Kansas Agricultural College, who was collaborating with MacDougal on a study of gases in wood. Another six scientists had worked at the laboratory in 1932. After that, though, several years elapsed before outsiders used the facilities again.

Instead of being the lively place Shreve had envisioned, full of scientists coming and going, the laboratory was a backwater, with just himself and his assistants. As he told Ellsworth Huntington, "things are going along very quietly at the Desert Laboratory these days, as the Institution does not seem to be able to expand its personnel at this direction." It was unfortunate, he wrote, "that we should not be able to develop more strongly the one desert station which is devoted to purely scientific work." He believed more than ever that the desert offered "a splendid field for work," and he was "increasingly impressed with the desirability of investigating the desert as a whole."[19] He added that, after normal economic conditions returned, he hoped to interest Merriam in a "larger program of work" for the laboratory.

In the meantime, travel at least was cheap. In March 1930 Shreve and four other scientists had made a week-long field trip to northwestern Sonora for only $110.49, which paid for food, gas, the services of a driver and cook, and customs duty on evaporated milk, oil, and gasoline.[20] Two years later, Shreve traveled again in Sonora on his fourth trip to Mexico. LeRoy Abrams, plant taxonomist at Stanford University and one of the foremost botanists on the West Coast, accompanied him. Their itinerary took them through the Magdalena and San Miguel river valleys to Hermosillo and south to Guaymas.

As Shreve wrote to Merriam beforehand, he hoped to secure "data on the habitats occupied by *Covillea*, *Fouquieria*, *Parkinsonia*, and *Encelia*, forms to which we have been giving special attention in our work at the Desert Laboratory."[21] Abrams was interested in making an extended plant collection. From this inconspicuous beginning came Shreve's best-known work, his study of the vegetation of the Sonoran Desert.[22]

After the trip Shreve told Merriam that Abrams's interest in the floristics of the region and his own in its vegetation and ecology were closely parallel. Shreve hoped they could continue their cooperation "in the direction of a survey of the floristic and ecological plant geography of southern California, southern Arizona, northern Sonora, and northern Lower California." Such a study "would be an important cornerstone on which to build a knowledge of the history and development of the North American desert."[23]

By September he had a preliminary research plan ready for Abrams and Spoehr's approval. Shreve would study the vegetation and ecology of the Sonoran Desert, and Abrams would prepare the flora. Hard-pressed by Spoehr and Merriam to come up with a vigorous, visionary research program, Shreve may have hoped that this would fill the bill. Although he still believed that "the essence of ecological work lies in the relation of organisms to the environment rather than in floristic geographical and descriptive work,"[24] he was to spend the next five years describing the vegetation of the Sonoran Desert.

Abrams soon decided that he was too busy writing his *Illustrated Flora of the Pacific States* to take an active part in the project, and he recommended Ira L. Wiggins, a young taxonomist at Stanford, to take his place. Wiggins was already working on a floristic study of Baja California, and he would be able to devote most of his research time to the Sonoran Desert project. Shreve concurred, and in October he and Wiggins traveled to Puerto Libertad.

Understanding Desert Life

The Sonoran Desert project had a shaky start financially. Shreve believed that he could complete the ecological work in five years, but Merriam refused to commit funds that far in advance. Even so, Shreve told Abrams, "there is every good reason for us to proceed with the investigation during the next two years in confidence that it will be possible for us to see it through."[1]

The more Shreve thought about his new project, the bigger it became. In January 1933 he explained his plans to Merriam: "As I now visualize our project for investigation of the desert from the dynamic and historical aspect, I can see five lines of work calculated to furnish evidence." The first was Abrams's taxonomic studies, the second, Shreve's ecological investigations. Studies of paleontology and physiography, in which he hoped Ralph Chaney and Eliot Blackwelder would participate, were to be the third line of investigation. Fourth, Duncan Johnson and E. J. Kraus would begin morphological studies of certain desert plants. The stelar anatomy of *Fouquieria, Idria,* and representative cacti would be the fifth aspect of the project. Shreve believed that "important contributions can be made by each of these lines of investigation, that the workers in them can be of great aid to each other, and that much sounder conclusions will result from as broad an attack on the problem as it is possible to make."[2]

Much of the project depended on fieldwork. The only way to describe the vegetation of the Sonoran Desert accurately was to see it firsthand, and over the course of the project Shreve logged ten thousand miles throughout the region. The pace of these trips was deliberate. Due to poor roads and frequent stops for collecting plants and making notes, Shreve and his companions often traveled no more than forty or fifty miles a day. At almost every stop, Shreve unpacked his camera and sauntered around until he found a suitable spot for a photograph of the vegetation. He used a heavy bellows camera that required glass plate negatives, and operating it called for patience and skill. In the late afternoon, the party began to look for a campsite—a place with plenty of firewood and room for sleeping bags. Shreve would say, "Well, maybe we'd better get things ready," and someone would wrap a bottle of tequila in a wet towel and hold it out the window as they drove to cool it off.[3] At the campsite Shreve would ceremoniously pass the bottle, "the best solution," as Wiggins put it, "for abolishing fatigue, removing desert dust from tonsils, and overcoming differences of opinion and misunderstandings."[4] Then they disassembled the plant presses and dried the blotters around the fire.

By the thirties, travel in Arizona had become easy and popular. Shreve noted "a marked change in the prevailing attitude towards deserts . . . largely due to the fact that they may now be visited easily and comfortably without any of the perils which used to attend any journeys through them. The automobile is undoubtedly responsible for this change to a great extent."[5] Travel in Sonora was not so easy, however. Even as late as 1937, major roads were unimproved, and some were little more than trails. Others were deeply rutted, parallel tracks. Because Shreve's Willys Knight could straddle the high centers of such roads, he kept it for fieldwork long after lower, sleeker cars were in fashion. To protect the car from overhanging brush, he had a canvas cover made that shielded the boxlike body, leaving only the windshield and part of the hood exposed.

Shreve usually traveled with two vehicles in case one broke down.

Forrest Shreve and daughter Margaret beside the Willys Knight

Fortunately, Mallery was an ingenious mechanic, and his improvisations and foresight saved them several times. Mallery later recalled that during one trip through Baja California he suddenly realized that one of his wheels was rolling down the road ahead of him. The axle was broken but disaster was averted because, on the advice of a friend, Mallery had brought along a replacement. He noted later that, during the two days it took him to install the new axle, not a single person passed by.[6]

Supplies of food and water were uncertain across much of Sonora. Natural tanks of water in bedrock streambeds were rare and could not be relied on. Shreve regarded the water from wells in remote settlements with "grave suspicion."[7] Usually they took water from Tucson and used it sparingly. Mallery told of seeing Shreve "take a cup of water, wash his face, clean his teeth, and pour the remainder in Willys's radiator."[8] As camp cook, Mallery planned the meals and shopped for food. Occasionally they supplemented their stock of food with beans, eggs, meat, and cornmeal purchased along the way. When the opportunity arose, Wiggins and Mallery fished in the Gulf of California. Mallery took a rifle on most trips and sometimes shot deer or javelina. One time a more unusual animal made an impromptu appearance on the menu: while Wiggins was collecting firewood in the evening, a rattler struck at him and embedded its fangs in his boot. After Wiggins killed the snake, Turnage skinned it, then roasted it over the campfire. Mallery later noted that although the flavor was comparable to chicken or pork, no one complained when roast rattler failed to appear at later meals.[9]

Weather occasionally posed problems. On a trip through Baja California in 1935 it rained almost daily for several weeks. Mallery had brought along chains for one of the cars, but Shreve had failed to bring a set for his Willys Knight. Even with chains, travel was nearly impossible over the clay roads. The entire party holed up in El Rosario for five days, waiting for the rain to abate. Although Shreve, in his diary for February 7, laconically noted, "there was a hard rain in the night but we all slept dry," Wiggins later recalled:

> The four of us, Shreve, Mallery, [Jack] Whitehead, and I, were able to keep dry in a leaky room of the Espinosas' home by arranging Shreve's and Mallery's cots at right angles against two walls, and Whitehead and I rolled our sleeping bags parallel to Mallery's cot, with the feet of our bags under Shreve's cot. Three tin cans were set beneath leaks between Jacks's and my sleeping bags. We spent four nights like that.[10]

Finally, the rains let up enough that they could creep onward to El Marmol, where they had to wait another five days before they could go farther south.

Sometimes personal problems interfered with the smooth running of the project. Wiggins was intermittently ill, then tied up with a heavy teaching schedule. Shreve himself came down with malaria in the fall of 1934, and his doctor confined him to bed for most of October. The following month he was still too sick to make his usual trip to the East Coast for the annual meeting of the Carnegie Institution.

The depression continually intruded on their plans, too. In 1933 Merriam would not commit himself to funding the Sonoran Desert project beyond 1935. Instead, he encouraged Shreve to accomplish as much as possible under the regular appropriation. Spoehr warned in August 1934 that "it is going to be extremely difficult to adjust budgets during the coming year, but we shall of course do everything to advance your main program of the study of the Sonoran desert."[11] Shreve replied that he had increased his budget request for travel from $1,000 to $1,200 only because he planned to carry on more fieldwork. He pointed out, "The more advanced our work becomes on the Sonoran Desert the more difficult is the country covered in our field trips and the heavier is the expense of travel."[12] By September 1935 he had exhausted his travel budget and could not make any long trips until the start of the next fiscal year. Wiggins's work on the flora proceeded more slowly than Shreve's on the vegetation, and even after Shreve finished his part of the work, Wiggins still needed to visit various herbaria on the East Coast and abroad. Because of the deepening depression, he could not obtain funds for these trips from Stanford University. Although not much of a politician, Shreve was able to secure appropriations from the institution for several of Wiggins's trips.

The first official field trip of the project in April 1933 was followed by nine others over the next five years. Although the total number of trips was not large, most of them lasted at least two weeks, many longer. One expedition to the tip of Baja California took sixty-five days. Each excursion provided new sights, new plants, new knowledge, new data, all of which Shreve worked and reworked into his gestalt of the Sonoran Desert.

On the April 1933 trip to the Yaqui and Mayo rivers in southern Sonora, Shreve observed for the first time the transition from desert vegetation to thornscrub. A train trip to Mazatlán in December enabled him to examine thornscrub more closely. The transition between thornscrub and desert occurred in southern Sonora over a distance of two hundred kilometers, Shreve noted in "Vegetation of the Northwest Coast of Mexico." Although desert vegetation extended far to the north and thornscrub far to the south, the transition between the two was narrow. To Shreve, this suggested "the operation of a potent group of controlling conditions," among them summer rainfall and frost.[13] He noted that desert plants in southwestern Arizona were both drought-resistant and cold-resistant, whereas thornscrub plants in Sinaloa were drought-resistant only.

Ferrying across the Río Yaqui

He concluded that "winter temperature conditions have strongly limited the number of drought resistant plants that have been able to enter the desert, and that the relatively small flora of the desert is not to be attributed solely to adverse moisture conditions."[14]

Soon after the April trip to southern Sonora, Shreve and Mallery traveled through southern Yuma County in Arizona. Shreve was glad for the chance to see the northernmost part of the Sonoran Desert while his impressions of the southernmost section were still fresh. Particularly noteworthy was "the gradual thinning of the vegetation and also the rapid impoverishment of the flora." He observed that "the genera and vegetative types which are represented by several, or even by numerous species in the south are found to contribute only a single species or type in the north." It was easy to see how greatly "the moist tropics of America have contributed the plants that have colonized the desert."[15] Other trips in 1933 included the usual biennial trek along the Camino del Diablo to read the long-period rain gauges, and an excursion through Barstow, Las Vegas, Boulder Dam, Chloride, Kingman, and Congress Junction. Here Shreve realized that he needed to modify his preliminary map of the

Sonoran Desert; he had shown it extending too far north along the Big Sandy River in northwestern Arizona.

Shreve's delineation of the Sonoran Desert and its subdivisions has become entrenched in the popular and scientific literature of the Southwest. Most lay people and many scientists still use his treatment with little modification. When Shreve began the project, however, knowledge of North American deserts, particularly in Mexico, was meager. There was no consensus as to their outlines or their names. The terms *Mojave Desert*, *Colorado Desert*, *Gulf Desert*, and *Sonoran Desert* were used more in a geographical sense than in a biological one. In 1924 Shreve had thought of northeastern Baja California as the Gulf Desert and southeastern California as the Colorado Desert. He had also suggested that the term *Sonoran Desert* be applied to the area that extended from central Arizona west to the Colorado River and south to the Gulf of California. By 1933, however, he had decided that the Sonoran Desert included parts of Arizona, Sonora, and Baja California between 27° and 35° latitude and from sea level to 3,500 feet, and he drew a preliminary map for use in his investigations. In July 1934 he drew a second map, this time showing vegetational subdivisions. "I am quite certain that this will need modification as our work continues," he told Abrams, and he was correct.[16] By 1937 Shreve had probably arrived at his final delineation of the desert and its subdivisions.

After the first year of fieldwork Shreve calculated that he had traveled more than twenty-six hundred miles in the deserts of Arizona and Sonora. Perhaps to clarify his thoughts after so much travel and so many new plants, he wrote "The Problems of the Desert," a paper he described as "a statement of my motivating philosophy with reference to our work here."[17] His first year of work had clearly demonstrated that the study of deserts was complex. To have a full understanding of the problems of the desert, he wrote, a scientist should investigate physiographic processes, climatic influences, distribution and character of groundwater and soils, plant structure, stream regimen, animal behavior, and human culture. "Every aspect of the desert is closely tied to every other aspect of it,"[18] he said in developing his argument for a holistic approach to desert research.

"An understanding of desert life cannot be built up by the employment of any one restricted method or procedure" but should involve outlooks from the "entire range of biological science." The viewpoint of the old-fashioned naturalist would be helpful for understanding life histories and behavior of animals. Their distribution should be studied in relation to environmental conditions, and further, "the study of structure must accompany the investigation of function" and "the study of function must lean heavily on the physical sciences."[19]

After a year of fieldwork in Sonora and thirty years of research in Tucson, Shreve could state his aims as a series of questions. Where did Sonoran Desert plants come from? How did the endemics originate? How did migration into the desert and evolution interact? Had any ancient desert taxa invaded moister regions? His objective was no longer simply to describe plant communities but to study vegetation and flora for clues to the origin of the desert.

In February and March 1934 Shreve traveled the Baja California peninsula as far south as Bahia Concepción. He discovered that "there is not only the well known difference between the flora on the two sides of the Gulf, but there is even a greater difference in the vegetation. The great majority of the dominant plants of Lower California are either absent or sparingly represented in Sonora." The difference in vegetation made it obvious that physical conditions in Lower California were "more severe than in Sonora or Arizona, particularly with respect to the length of drought periods." The contrast in flora and climate presented "a chain of problems of absorbing interest."[20]

After a trip to northeastern Sonora in October 1934, Shreve admitted that a number of his "preconceived opinions about the vegetation were wholly wrong." Unexpectedly, he had discovered that the interior valleys were quite unlike the region that extends from Tucson to Hermosillo. "In these valleys and the adjacent hills," he wrote, "the vegetation is very open but contains many of the familiar elements that characterize the thorn forest further south."[21]

In February and March of 1935 Shreve made another trip to Baja California. He and his companions "followed the one and only road the full length of the peninsula, and found it possible to make side trips by car and on foot which gave us fine cross sections at different latitudes, in addition to which we circled the Cape District south of La Paz." From La Paz they took a small boat to Guaymas, "skirting the coast as far north as Loreto and getting a fine panorama of the rugged slopes which are difficult of access from the interior." Shreve and Wiggins had considerable discussion about where the southern limit of the desert occurred. Shreve said that his idea of desert was "based on the height of the plants, density of stand, and the types of life forms comprised." Wiggins's concept was based on plant families and genera, which, Shreve insisted, "is floristics and not ecology." They agreed that most of the Cape District was not desert from either standpoint. "However," Shreve wrote, "from my own point of view, practically all of the volcanic country on the east side of the Cape District, all of the Magdalena Plain and nearly all of the country between Santa Rosalia and Comondu is just as truly desert as any part of the peninsula."[22]

While they were storm-bound in El Marmol for five days, Shreve "blocked out a paper on the transition from desert to chaparral along the northwestern coast of Lower California." He had noticed that the change from chaparral around Tijuana to desert at El Rosario was "spread over a distance of 200 miles," whereas the same transition occupied fewer than twenty miles in California's San Gorgonio Pass. The "gradual but profound" changes in flora and vegetation found with decreasing latitude made him realize that the tip of Baja California was "just as isolated as if it were an island."[23]

Shreve observed on this trip that chaparral plants penetrated farther into the desert than desert plants did into the chaparral. He concluded that "the only requirement for the long southward extension of a chaparral plant is the occurrence in the desert region of relatively moist habitats, however restricted in area." In contrast, "the northward extension of a desert plant requires a well-drained soil, a high percentage of sunshine, and freedom from freezing temperatures of more than a few hours' duration."[24]

Shreve explained his fascination with transitions between major formations—between desert and chaparral, desert and thornscrub, desert and grassland—in "The Edge of the Desert," published in 1940. He wrote, "The physiologist and the ecologist are equally interested in two critical sets of conditions: those that represent the optimum for the plant and those that constitute the limiting margin of its existence. It is for these reasons that the ecologist is interested in both the center of his region and in the edge of his region."[25]

In March 1936 Shreve visited northwestern Sonora and western Arizona with Mallery, Wiggins, and plant taxonomist David Keck, a trip he referred to as "filling in the gaps." The region was "chiefly a vast sandy plain, broken in the vicinity of Pinacate Peak by a volcanic field which extends from 6 to 28 miles from the peak." Because the area had been "almost wholly formed by volcanic disturbances and by the action of wind on the sandy surface," it made a strong contrast to the rest of the Sonoran Desert, "in which rain and streams have been the chief agencies in shaping the topography." Shreve remarked on the "highly unfavorable conditions for plants, as well as for man." He was greatly interested "to find large areas in which the plant communities are reduced in their composition to only three species of perennials, and other areas, indeed, in which small widely spaced creosote bushes were the only perennials."[26]

The more time Shreve spent traveling in the Sonoran Desert, the broader his viewpoint became and the more his interest in the origin and history of the desert intensified. In "Plant Life of the Sonoran Desert," published in 1936, he said, "The most important aim of our work is to keep in view the vast array of influences and circumstances that have determined the history of desert plants and now determine the life and survival of every one of them."[27]

Shreve saw the different life forms of desert plants—the elephant-trunked trees of Sonora and Baja, the succulent-stemmed cacti, the many-stemmed shrubs, the drought-deciduous trees, the short-lived wildflowers and grasses—in evolutionary terms. The diversity of life forms was "an indication of the numerous ways in which evolutionary development has worked out solutions for the problem of life in the desert."[28] Plants in moist regions were forced through competition to assume the single life form best suited to their climate. In tropical rain forests, for example, the dominant life form was the evergreen, broad-leaved tree. In deserts, however, many different life forms had been able to evolve because plants struggled not with each other but with the environment.

Shreve's interest in life forms was long-standing. In 1921 he had objected to Raunkiauer's life-form classification because it did not adequately reflect plant physiology in relation to environment. He recommended instead Drude's classification system, which used "criteria to which a definite physiological importance can be ascribed."[29] Seventeen years later he still believed that a life-form classification should be "a rough physiological classification of the plants irrespective of their phylogenetic relationship."[30]

In "Plant Life of the Sonoran Desert" Shreve speculated that desert plants had migrated in response to fluctuations of temperature and rainfall during the Pleistocene. He had spent some time over the last six years preparing distribution maps of certain species, and these maps, along with his field observations, showed four possible migrational routes—a coastal path, a peninsular path, a foothill path, and a mountain path. Along these paths he discerned "chains" of related species whose distribution overlapped little or not at all. Such chains—he used barrel cacti and prickly pears as examples—combined evidence of both migratory movement and evolutionary activity, and appeared to be relatively recent. He concluded, "The inference is strong that in such groups as *Ferocactus* and *Opuntia* there has been steady movement accompanied by the appearance of new species and that these phenomena have taken place in very recent times in the geologic sense." Broken chains indicated "cases in which the genus or species has lost some of the general ground which it formerly occupied. . . . The evidence suggests that these plants belong to an older wave of movement."[31] Perhaps some of them had even endured the climatic shifts of the Pleistocene in situ.

Shreve's renewed interest in climatic change may have been sparked by fossil discoveries. In 1933 Chester Stock, a vertebrate paleontologist and a colleague of Shreve's within the Carnegie Institution, became curious about plant fragments found in fossilized sloth dung from

Gypsum Cave near Las Vegas, Nevada. At J. C. Merriam's suggestion, Shreve examined the dung to identify the plants. He later told Merriam that "it is not going to be possible to make specific determinations of any of the plants involved but a good deal can be inferred as to the climatic conditions under which these food plants lived from the character of the leaf fragments." Without hesitation, he suggested that the sloths had fed upon plants that required much more water than those currently in the vicinity of Gypsum Cave. He based his conclusion on the anatomical structure of the leaf fragments, which were thin and provided with numerous stomata, unlike leaves of characteristic desert plants. Many of the fragments, he believed, were moss leaves. "If I am correct in my interpretation," Shreve told Merriam, "these fragments . . . would indicate a rainfall of not less than 75 inches per annum."[32]

Just five months later he visited J. D. Laudermilk, a paleontologist at Pomona College in Claremont, California, who had taken over the investigation of the dung specimens. To his chagrin, Shreve learned that Laudermilk had determined that the plant fragments consisted mostly of Joshua tree and desert holly, both desert plants able to survive on much less rain than seventy-five inches. Shreve could only conclude that "there is a botanical importance in the confirmation of the existence in late Pleistocene of the same plants now found in southern Nevada."[33] He had not yet recognized the true importance of the discovery, which depended on the fact that, although Joshua tree no longer grew in the vicinity of Gypsum Cave, it was plentiful nearby at somewhat higher elevations. Its range had contracted since the time when ground sloths inhabited Gypsum Cave, indicating, as Laudermilk and Munz stated, that the climate had become increasingly dry since then.[34] This experience, mortifying as it may have been, was not wasted on Shreve; three years later he was attempting to integrate the new findings into his own hypotheses.

Shreve believed that the arid conditions of the desert had favored evolution. The cactus family, which had apparently originated in tropical America, was one example. He postulated that as cacti had migrated from the tropics into the desert, the arid conditions they encountered had contributed to their marked speciation. "Only certain types of the family have been highly successful as migrants," he wrote, "but those types have broken into a very large number of species which are now massed along the advanced frontier."[35] Anatomical studies might clarify evolutionary relationships within the cactus family, Shreve thought. He was "particularly interested in the possibility of learning more about the relation between the Cactaceae and the Loasaceae as well as securing some reference on the relationship of the Fouquieriaceae."[36]

His interest in the phylogeny of desert plants led him to study the genus *Franseria* (now *Ambrosia*), the small shrubs commonly called bursage. He looked at the group from several angles—taxonomic, ecological, and distributional. For his taxonomic monograph of the bursages, Shreve consulted eleven herbaria in nine states over a period of several years. He recognized twenty-seven species in the genus and reduced to synonymy twelve of the thirty-nine previously recognized by Per Rydberg. More interesting to him than the taxonomy of the bursages was their distribution and ecological relationships. Fourteen of the thirty-nine were restricted to the Sonoran Desert, and Shreve noted that "the area of maximum speciation and abundance of *Franseria* coincides closely with the part of the Sonoran Desert which has winter rainfall."[37] He evidently intended to publish his *Ambrosia* monograph in *Die Pflanzenareale*, a German geographical journal, but the outbreak of World War II made that impracticable. No doubt he also hoped that his taxonomic treatment would be used in his and Wiggins's book on vegetation and flora of the Sonoran Desert. But because of the delay in preparing the flora, the monograph was set aside and never published.

Although the *Ambrosia* monograph was Shreve's only foray into plant taxonomy, he did have a keen interest in and strong opinions about taxonomical problems. One time, according to C.H. Muller, Shreve reacted to Susan Stokes's monograph on the genus *Eriogonum* by throwing the book into the fireplace. Another time he remarked that his "feelings of pain and resentment were freshly stirred" each time a volume of Britton and Rose's monograph on the cactus family appeared; but, he added, "I always endeavor to quiet myself by the realization that I am not a systematical botanist and have no business to pass judgment on this work."[38]

In March 1937 Shreve made his last trip for the Sonoran Desert project when he traveled with Mallery through northwestern Arizona, the southern tip of Nevada, and along the Colorado River below Boulder Dam. His principal aim was "to endeavor to define more closely the boundaries between the Sonoran Desert and the Mohave and Great Basin types of desert." He felt satisfied that he had succeeded and added that "operations were greatly facilitated by the fact that there are now very good roads leading almost everywhere. The construction of Boulder Dam, the Parker Dam, the great power lines, and aqueduct have all led to the construction of good roads through country that was formerly accessible only with some difficulty."[39] It was time to bring the Sonoran Desert project to a close, even though, as he told Paul C. Standley in March 1937, he could spend another five years working there "with great profit."[40]

A Model and a Classic

News of Shreve's Sonoran Desert project spread beyond scientific circles throughout the thirties. The Carnegie Institution discovered that his field trips made good copy, and at the request of W. M. Gilbert, the institution's administrative secretary, Shreve wrote a series of press releases describing the project. He was interested to see "some of the difficulties which confront any effort to place reliable scientific information in the hands of the daily papers" and frustrated to discover there was "no way of preventing omission, addition, or change of emphasis."[1] In 1934, for example, the *New York Herald Tribune*, seeking to make a good story better, dramatically reported: "Cactus Found to Be Invading Species Migrating From Tropics Across Arizona to an Unknown Destination."[2] After every press release the Desert Laboratory was inundated with requests for copies of the article and "with letters from people of every shade of interest with comment and inquiries reaching all the way from the treatment of rattlesnake bites to the economic status of the desert."[3]

Every December the institution held an exhibit illustrating the research conducted by the various departments. In the hope of putting the Desert Laboratory "back on the map,"[4] Shreve outdid himself for the 1935 show. Starting six months ahead of time, he and Mallery constructed a relief model of the Sonoran Desert showing topography and major vegetational subdivisions. Shreve told Wiggins, "It has been necessary to do some pretty tall guessing with reference to the topography in Sonora, but I believe that the model will be sufficiently accurate for its purpose and will help to give us a graphic idea of the lay of the land."[5] He and Mallery even made a special trip to Puerto Libertad in November to dig up three boojum trees, which they shipped along with other live plants to Washington, D. C., as part of the exhibit.

On his annual trips to Washington, Shreve invariably visited colleagues in the East. He often worked at the major eastern herbaria, which then included the Smithsonian Institution, the U.S. National Herbarium, the New York Botanical Garden, and the National Academy of Science. His traveling schedule also included one or more trips every year to California to consult with Spoehr and other colleagues in Palo Alto, Berkeley, and Carmel. Shreve also attended annual scientific meetings, where he usually read at least one paper.

The late twenties and early thirties were a time of growing public interest in the desert. Ambitious developers hoping to capitalize on the growing tourist boom subdivided large tracts of land north and east of Tucson. As development accelerated, Shreve became concerned about preserving the desert. He pointed out that "we have devastated the original animal life of the southwest to such a point that we are now creating game sanctuaries in the hope of saving the remnants." Although the destruction of natural communities usually had economic necessity as its justification, in other cases it was "due to ill-advised efforts to push agriculture into areas where it can not be prosecuted with success." He noted that "many of the dry farms of Arizona have ruined the virgin grassland areas almost as completely as they have ruined the farmers themselves."[6]

The indiscriminate removal of desert vegetation for housing developments angered Shreve. He noted that well-established mesquite trees were cut down and exotics having little to recommend them planted in their stead. His objections came from an intimate understanding of how slowly desert plants grew and how intensely they had struggled with their environment to survive. "It requires only ten minutes to cut down a large palo verde tree," he said. "Such a tree has required from 200 to 300 years to reach mature size, and is the sole survivor of many thousands of palo verde seedlings that have made a start within 100 feet of it and have succumbed to the arid conditions."[7]

As more people "discovered" the desert, interest in cacti boomed. Shreve tried to focus some of this interest in a book on cacti for a popular audience. He began writing *The Cactus and Its Home* in 1927 and finally submitted it to Williams and Wilkins Company in 1931. They published it in December of that year.

Shreve had high hopes for the book. Thornber's *Sage of the Desert*, printed in an edition of 2,500 copies, had sold out in three months, and Shreve thought his own book might do as well. He was disappointed. In March 1932 his publishers notified him that, in the four months since the book had appeared, only 320 copies had sold. Shreve (like many authors) believed that the book was not being promoted properly. He complained that "the publishers have a great way of sending circulars by mail to many people but never do any advertising in papers or magazines."[8]

The book deserved a better fate. In five chapters Shreve explained the evolution, structure, taxonomy, ecology, and cultivation of cacti. His characteristic wit enlivened the text, and he addressed such concepts as natural selection and adaptation with a minimum of technical language. He did not condescend or pander to his audience, however. Some years earlier he had "spent hours in large book stores trying to find juvenile books about nature that were not sugar coated with the personification of wind, clouds, waves, rain, trees, and mountains, or books about animals in which they were not dressed in skirts or trousers and endowed with the ability to express their human ideas." He believed that nothing was more interesting than "nature itself, without gloss, refinement, or distortion."[9]

In *The Cactus and Its Home* Shreve debunked the teleological idea that cactus spines evolved to protect the plants from animals. "It would be difficult," he said, "to find a competent biologist who would maintain that the less spiny plants were eaten and the more spiny ones protected and preserved, and that for these reasons the members of the cactus family gradually procured their characteristic spininess." He went on to point out that it was much more probable that "the development of spines is a direct physiological effect of the dry atmosphere and scanty water supply."[10] Once spines had evolved, it turned out that they also served to protect cacti from thirsty or hungry animals. Just as in Jamaica more than twenty years before, he was trying to cure ecology of teleological tendencies.

Physiological ecologists have since demonstrated that spines do indeed serve a physiological function, as Shreve had suspected. In modeling the effect of cactus spines on the temperature of the growing stem tip, Park S. Nobel has found that the spines of a pincushion cactus reduce the risk of overheating on the hottest days and of freezing during the coldest nights. Spine density is an important factor in preventing frost damage to the tender meristematic tissue at the apex of the barrel cactus, also.[11]

Although Shreve did not profit from the current fad for cactus, the spiny succulents proved lucrative for others. Collectors were devastating cactus populations in Arizona and California and selling the plants to cactus fanciers. Arizona's first native plant protection law, passed in 1929, proved inadequate, and Shreve, along with other concerned botanists, pushed for a more effective one. He told the speaker of the state House of Representatives that he had seen "a great deal of the despoiling of our native flora, especially in the southern part of the state."[12] In fact, as he told another correspondent, "it is very evident throughout southern Yuma County that everything in the cactus line has been picked out."[13] In 1933 an amendment was passed that made it harder to remove protected plants from private property and easier to prosecute violators of the law.

In 1932 Shreve served as president of the Tucson Natural History Society. Founded in 1923 by animal ecologist Walter P. Taylor, the society met once a month and made regular excursions to points of interest in southern Arizona. Various biologists conducted the trips and gave informal talks. The aim of the society was not only to encourage nature appreciation but also to stimulate recognition of "the great need for measures of conservation."[14] One of its early achievements was persuading the U.S. Forest Service to establish a natural area in the Santa Catalina Mountains.

Shreve believed that the desert was "a breathing place for those who are fortunate enough to be able to get away, either permanently or temporarily, from the crowded centers of population,"[15] and along with other members of the society, he worked to have large tracts of desert land set aside as natural preserves. In 1932 he visited several potential sites for national monuments with Roger Toll, the superintendent of Yellowstone National Park. Toll was particularly interested in areas that would "perpetuate a fine display of Carnegiea and other cacti,"[16] and at Shreve's suggestion they visited suitable areas in southern Arizona, including the western base of the Rincon Mountains, where Saguaro National Monument was established in 1933. In the same year the Tucson Natural History Society passed a resolution favoring the creation of a national monument south of Ajo on the west side of the Ajo Mountains; partly as a result of their efforts, Organ Pipe Cactus National Monument was established there in 1937.

The Sonoran Desert project revived Shreve's interest in plant collecting. In 1929 he had told one correspondent, "It has been a number of years since I have collected any plants and am not sure that I will be able to assist you very much with herbarium materials."[17] But once he began traveling in the field with Ira Wiggins, he made many collections, and every excursion in Arizona, California, or Sonora—even family vacations—provided an excuse to collect plants. Usually Shreve sent his specimens to experts for identification: as he told Paul Standley, "my lack of training, comparative material, and adequate literature makes it necessary for me to lean heavily on other people in these matters."[18] A small proportion of his collections proved to be new species, and at least ten of them were named after him, including *Agave shrevei, Fouquieria shrevei*, and *Brongniartia shrevei*.

By 1944 Shreve had collected or purchased some thirty thousand specimens. His herbarium held sets of "nearly all of the important collections that have been made in Mexico since 1930"[19] and represented many of the famous early plant collectors—Cyrus G. Pringle,

Edward Palmer, Marcus E. Jones, and Joseph A. Purpus. Plants of Mexico comprised about half the collection; most of the remainder came from the southwestern United States.

Maintaining such a sizable collection was difficult. In 1935 Shreve told C. E. Lundell not to hurry in sending some five hundred specimens because "I am already over 2,000 numbers behind the game in mounting and distributing material on hand."[20] Money for purchasing collections and maintaining the herbarium came from Shreve's own pocket since his budget made no provision for such expenses.

About a year before he retired, Shreve offered to sell his herbarium to the University of Arizona for what it had cost him to assemble it—about $2,500. Lyman Benson, then assistant professor of botany, recommended strongly that the university buy Shreve's collection, which he called "one of the finest representations of the Mexican flora in existence."[21] The university bought the herbarium in 1944.

Another offshoot of the Sonoran Desert project was Shreve's living collection of desert plants. As he traveled in Sonora, he collected live plants and seeds of many different species. The plants, which he placed in the cactus garden at the Desert Laboratory, included the boojum tree, a tree ocotillo named after D. T. MacDougal, and many cacti—pincushions, senitas, organ pipes, prickly pears, and others.

From 1933 to 1938 Shreve had Mallery grow more than ninety species of Sonoran Desert plants from seed in the laboratory greenhouse. They discovered that nearly half the species required special treatment in order to germinate. Seeds of the large perennials germinated best when soil temperatures were between 80° and 95°F, the prevailing range during the summer rainy season. Shreve was curious about the germination of ephemerals as well, and with the cooperation of the Boyce Thompson Institute in Yonkers, New York, confirmed his hypothesis "that the seasonal appearance of summer and winter annuals in the Tucson region is due to differences in the range of their optimum temperature requirements."[22]

Early in the Sonoran Desert project Shreve had become interested in the ranges of certain Sonoran Desert plants, and between 1931 and 1935 he prepared distributional maps of palo verde, ironwood, saguaro, and many other trees and shrubs. Field observations and herbarium labels provided the data for these maps, which he published in *Die Pflanzenareale* and *Vegetation of the Sonoran Desert*. As always, his geographical and ecological interests were tightly bound. The study of plant distribution for its own sake did not appeal to him, though; he invariably sought to correlate it with environmental variables.

During 1938 and 1939 Shreve wove it all together. The work on seed germination, the ten thousand miles of field trips, the hundreds of collections, the climatic data, the measurements of soil moisture and temperature, the work on creosote bush, the maps of plant distribution—all this and much more became part of his classic book on the Sonoran Desert.

Although Shreve began "constructing the framework" of *Vegetation of the Sonoran Desert* in 1936,[23] he did not begin writing it until 1938.[24] Internal evidence suggests that the book was essentially completed in 1939. It seems likely that, once Shreve had finished the manuscript, he set it aside until Ira Wiggins could finish the flora. But various other projects and World War II intervened, and Wiggins did not complete his part of the project until 1964. In 1950, probably aware that he had little time left to live, Shreve resumed work on the manuscript, adding a few references and revising the text. The Carnegie Institution published *Vegetation of the Sonoran Desert* in 1951, the year after Shreve's death. Ecologist Frank Egler called it "a model and a classic" and commented, "I constantly wish that its author had given us a volume 10 times its size, with regional details that now may largely be lost."[25]

In the book's five chapters, Shreve discussed physical conditions of the Sonoran Desert, perennial vegetation, herbaceous ephemerals, and ecological features of characteristic species. Although he returned to familiar topics, most of the material had never been published before. The descriptions of vegetation, which took up more than half the book, were new. So were the lists of winter and summer ephemerals, the discussion of their germination requirements, and notes on their distribution.

Vegetation of the Sonoran Desert is best known for its division of

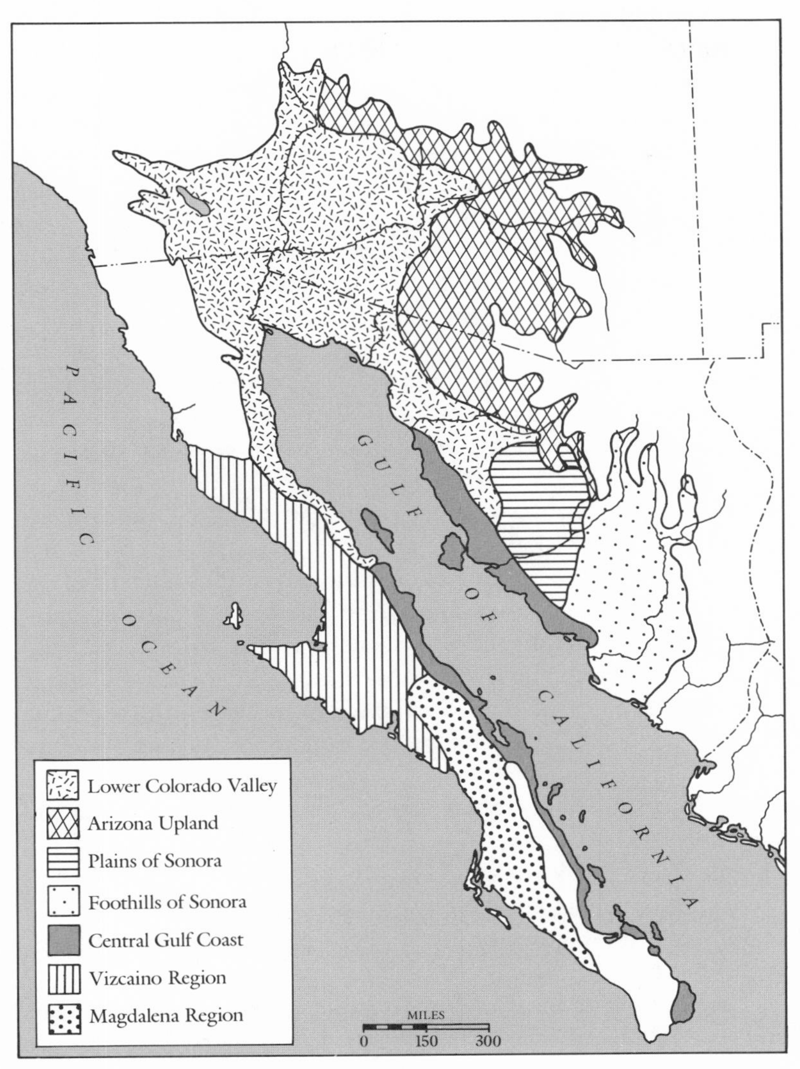

Seven regions of the Sonoran Desert first delineated, named, and described by Forrest Shreve (after Shreve 1951)

the desert into seven regions on the basis of vegetation. Shreve noted again that "the custom of using the habitat as part of the characterization of a plant community is an illogical procedure."[26] As before, his criteria were largely physiognomic: growth form, degree of openness, species richness. He devised three names for each subdivision: one that described the character of the vegetation, a second that indicated the dominant plant genera, and a third that designated the location or an outstanding geographical feature. Shreve used the geographical names in preference to the vegetational or floristic ones, and most scientists have done the same since.

According to Shreve, the "strongest impressions given by the vegetation of the Lower Colorado Valley are of uniformity over wide areas, and simplicity of composition." Creosote bush and white bursage dominated much of the region, no matter what the substrate, showing that "no other shrubs have developed biological and physiological characteristics so highly suited to survival"[27] in this extremely arid subdivision.

In contrast, a variety of trees, shrubs, and cacti characterized the Arizona Upland subdivision, including palo verde, ironwood, mesquite, creosote bush, brittlebush, saguaro, cholla, barrel cactus, and prickly pear. Throughout the subdivision, "differentiation of the vegetation is to be attributed to gradient of slope, depth of soil, physical texture of soil, and surface conditions affecting infiltration."[28]

The Plains of Sonora, Shreve noted, "constituted the smallest and least diversified of the vegetation subdivisions of the Sonoran Desert." Dominated by small trees such as ironwood, palo verde, and mesquite, and large columnar cacti such as organ pipe and senita, the region gave the impression of "a very open forest of small, low-branching trees."[29]

The Foothills of Sonora was the least desertlike of the subdivisions and, at its southern end, gradually gave way to thorn forest. Shreve placed the desert boundary "between the lower courses of the Río Yaqui and the Río Mayo, approximately at the place where vegetation with many open spaces gives way to a continuous cover of summer-green trees."[30] The thorn forest contributed heavily to the foothills flora, and many plant species in this subdivision grew in none of the others.

The Central Gulf Coast subdivision, like the Lower Colorado Valley, was a region of low and uncertain rainfall. Its characteristic plants—elephant tree, limber bush, and torchwood, among others—had swollen, water-storing trunks and were low in stature.

The Vizcaino Region, in central Baja California, was a desert of extremes. In some parts the vegetation was relatively dense and rich in species; in others it was sparse and impoverished. The features that controlled these extremes—and the shades of difference between them—were physiography, proximity to the sea, substrate, altitude, water supply, and slope aspect. Yucca and century plant, the representative species, had succulent leaves.

Much of the Magdalena Region was a coastal plain with deep, silty soils where small trees and columnar cacti grew in thickets. Elsewhere, a sparse covering of shrubs, small trees, and cacti found a foothold on the broken surface of volcanic mesas and malpais.

Not all plant ecologists have agreed with every aspect of Shreve's treatment of Sonoran Desert vegetation. Some have even asked whether much of the area can actually be called desert. Shreve would have been familiar with this objection, having met it as early as 1913, when a group of ten European botanists visited the Desert Laboratory. Many of them had worked in Old World deserts and were surprised to find that the Americans considered the relatively lush vegetation around Tucson to be desert. W. Robyns later complained that "Shreve had shown him a flower garden in 1913 and called it a desert!"[31] A. G. Tansley called the area a semidesert because "it has a distinct summer rainfall pattern in addition to the winter period and is thus climatically different from 'true' desert. Correspondingly the vegetation is more luxuriant and much more numerous in individuals than is the case in the typical North African deserts."[32]

Shreve, however, having experienced the physical rigors of the North American deserts first hand, refused to back down. Criticisms such as Robyns's may have eventually led him to define as precisely as possible his concept of a desert. Although it must have been shaped by his childhood and youth in much wetter climates, it was not based on ignorance, for he had seen photographs and read descriptions of Old World deserts. Because Shreve viewed vegetation as a continuum, he was willing to accept a continuum in deserts, too, from the barren, stony plains of the Sahara to the rich vegetation on the bajadas of the Santa Catalina Mountains.

More recently, plant ecologist Raymond Turner and biologist David Brown have suggested that of Shreve's seven subdivisions only three—the Lower Colorado Valley, the Central Gulf Coast, and parts of the Vizcaino Region—should be called desert. The rest Turner and Brown would designate "depauperate thornscrub."[33] Shreve himself was probably troubled by the distinction between thornscrub (which he usually called thorn forest) and desert. He noted several times that the transition between them was subtle. The distinction became especially blurred in the southern part of the Foothills of Sonora. He wrote that "all the criteria of desert, constantly exemplified in the areas to the north, have become so weakly expressed that much of the hill vegetation in the southern foothills is more closely allied to thorn forest than it is to desert." In the Foothills of Sonora, he noted, "the percentage of cover is high, the stature of plants is consistently greater, and the diversity of life forms is very much less."[34] The one compelling reason for calling the area desert rather than thorn forest was that he could easily walk through the vegetation in any direction. This was, perhaps, a graphic way of saying that the plants were more intensely involved in a struggle with their environment than with each other.

Shreve may have hoped that *Vegetation of the Sonoran Desert* would serve as a rebuttal to Clements's 1936 paper on North American deserts, "The Origin of the Desert Climax and Climate." Clements had defined a desert as an area marked by "the absence of forest or grassland, a critical deficit in rainfall, and a high potential evaporation caused by excessive heat and often by high winds also." According to him, deserts in North America occurred where annual rainfall was five inches or less. He vaguely described this region as being "confined to the Death Valley, Mohave and Colorado regions and to a larger but less known area in Mexico."[35]

Shreve's definition was more complex, reflecting his years of desert experience. His concept of desert had deepened since 1921, when he and Livingston had determined that the desert lands of the United States corresponded to the region where evaporation exceeded precipitation by five times. In *Vegetation of the Sonoran Desert* he emphasized that no single criterion would serve to define a desert in a biological or geographical sense. Rather, "a true characterization of desert must include evaluation of many variables,"[36] among them low and unevenly distributed rainfall, low humidity, high air temperature with great daily and seasonal ranges, high surface soil temperature, strong wind, soil with low content of organic matter and high content of mineral salts, violent erosional work by water and wind, and sporadic flow of streams. Accompanying these physical features were characteristic vegetational features: the plants do not form a closed cover, do not attain a "considerable size," do not grow throughout the year, and do not tolerate environmental conditions without considerable modification of physiology or morphology.

Although he wrote about the origin of the desert climax, Clements never worked in deserts long enough to discern actual successional patterns there. He even concluded that the desert's spring wildflowers represented "the pioneer stage of a succession which cannot develop further because of extreme conditions."[37] In 1920 he had stated that the community of saguaro, palo verde, and ocotillo was a subclimax, the next-to-last stage of succession that would eventually give way to creosote bush and bursage. Fourteen years later he contradicted this view by saying that saguaro, palo verde, and ocotillo had, as a result of human interference, replaced a grassland community; thus the vegetation was a postclimax, a stage that replaced the true climax.[38]

For Shreve, this shuffling of subclimax and postclimax was a distinction without a difference. As he told one correspondent, "I take very little interest in the formal treatment of vegetation and the customary descriptions of successions and climaxes treated with great attention to the formal and highly artificial classifications of which we have so many."[39] In *Vegetation of the Sonoran Desert* he reiterated that it "is not possible to use the term 'climax' with reference to desert vegetation. Each habitat in each subdivision has its own climax, which must be given an elastic definition and must not be interpreted as having a genetic relation to any other climax." Shreve insisted that the so-called desert climax was "merely the particular group of species which, in somewhat definite proportions and with a fairly definite communal arrangement, is able to occupy a particular location under its present environmental conditions."[40]

After thirty years of research, Shreve felt secure in stating once again that "the successional changes which are so important elsewhere may be read into the vegetation of the desert, but the evidence for them would hardly suggest that they are of importance in determining the relations of the communities to one another." As before, he noted that "if a particular community is destroyed without change in the soil, the earliest stage in the return of vegetation will be the appearance of young plants of the former dominants."[41] One reason for the absence of succession in the desert was "the almost total lack of reaction by the plant on its habitat," Shreve wrote in 1942. "Fallen leaves and twigs are blown away, or small accumulations of organic matter are washed away, to be carried ultimately to the nearest flood plain or playa." Thus the existence of a plant in a particular spot for many years did "nothing to make that spot a better habitat for some other plant or some other species." He concluded that "the succession concept would never have been developed in a study of the vegetation of arid regions."[42]

During the 1920s and 1930s, Shreve's ecological colleagues laid foundations for the theoretical, mathematical ecology that became ascendant in the 1970s. H. A. Gleason worked on species-area curves and quantification of plant sampling. Raymond Pearl made mathematical models of the growth of animal populations. A. J. Lotka considered mathematical formulations for parasite-host interactions. G. F. Gause modeled the principle that no two species living together can occupy the same ecological niche.[43]

While these ecologists were elaborating theories and formulating models, Shreve was delineating broad zones of vegetation, correlating vegetation with climate and substrate, and listing characteristic species. He must have been aware of the new trends, but apparently they held little interest for him. His early work in physiological ecology and plant geography had been rigorously theoretical for its time. In testing supposed adaptations of drip-tips, in pioneering in the field of plant population ecology, and in developing the continuum concept, Shreve showed himself capable of superb conceptual analysis. By the end of his career, though, Shreve was working on a more descriptive level, as the titles of the papers he published in the late 1930s and early 1940s show: "The Vegetation of the Cape Region of Baja California"; "Lowland Vegetation of Sinaloa"; "Observations on the Vegetation of Chihuahua"; "The Edge of the Desert"; "Grassland and Related Vegetation in Northern Mexico." Each of these papers, however, was a novel contribution. Little was known about the vegetation of northern Mexico until Shreve studied it. His synthesis of vegetation and physical environment provided a framework for subsequent generations of ecologists, biologists, and geographers. This is descriptive ecology at its best.

A Bitter Shock

Shreve intended *Vegetation of the Sonoran Desert* to be the first in a series of books about the North American deserts. For him, it was not a culmination but a beginning, and the next step was to study the vegetation and flora of the Chihuahuan Desert.

Shreve began thinking about a Chihuahuan Desert project in 1934, a few years after he started the Sonoran Desert project. As he explained to Merriam, "during the course of our work on the Sonoran Desert area I have been impressed with the results that might be secured by a similar investigation of the Chihuahuan Desert, lying in western Texas, Chihuahua, Coahuila, and parts of Nuevo Leon, Zacatecas, and San Luis Potosi." He suspected that the vegetation there was substantially different from that of the Sonoran Desert. Clearly, "the relations of vegetation and flora in the Chihuahuan and Sonoran Deserts would make the parallel investigation of the two of them much more fruitful than the study of either one alone."[1]

Before he wrote a formal proposal about the Chihuahuan Desert work, Shreve decided to preview the area. In July 1937 he and Mallery left for El Paso, where they met L. R. Dice, who planned to study mammals for the project. The three men spent most of their time in the state of Chihuahua, traveling fewer than one hundred miles a day.

Shreve discovered that conditions for car travel in Chihuahua were not as good as in Sonora because of the rough roads, rugged limestone terrain, and long distances between settlements. Having seen the terrain and the roads, he knew better how to plan the project. He believed it would be "easier and more economical to work a number of strategic points from railroad towns followed by automobile trips to regions which it then seemed desirable to traverse in greater detail."[2] He estimated that they could finish the vegetation part of the project in four years. The floristic part would undoubtedly take more time.

After this first trip, Shreve wrote a "brief sketch" of the vegetation of Chihuahua. He defined five physiographic regions—the Bajada Region, the Enclosed Basin Region, the Elevated Plains Region, the Sierra Madre Region, and the Barranca Region—and mapped four types of vegetation, which corresponded closely to the physiography. In describing the vegetation, he devoted the most space to the arid zone. The desert of Chihuahua, he wrote, "is a region of broad plains, long bajadas, and large basins with widely spaced ranges of low mountains." Though it was possible to travel as far as two hundred miles without encountering substantial differences in the vegetation, there were, nevertheless, marked changes from place to place. "The most distinct types of desert vegetation are those found in the sandy basins and dune region of the north, the bajadas and outwash plains of the northeast, the volcanic and limestone mountains of the northeast and east, the limestone plains of the south, and the bolsons of the southeast."[3] In its physiognomy the vegetation of Chihuahua was similar to that of southeastern Arizona and southwestern New Mexico, but floristically there was a "strong infusion of endemic or southern species not found in the United States."[4]

Shreve next visited the Chihuahuan Desert in August and September 1938. On a forty-three-day trip with Mallery and Ivan M. Johnston, the taxonomist for the project, he traveled through Coahuila into Zacatecas, San Luis Potosi, Durango, and north again through Chihuahua. By 1944 Shreve had made four more trips,

Forrest Shreve in the field about 1940

extending his coverage to the states of Aguascalientes, Hidalgo, Jalisco, and Queretaro.

His early impression was that in the Chihuahuan Desert "differences of elevation have less influence on the makeup of the vegetation than in the Sonoran Desert."[5] Additional fieldwork confirmed this impression. He concluded that "the distribution of vegetation in the Chihuahuan Desert is mainly controlled by the character of underlying rock and soil and by the major topographic features." Only at elevations of 1,000 to 2,000 feet above the surrounding plains did "the influence of climatic conditions become important in differentiating the vegetation."[6]

Had Shreve continued work on the project, he might not have subdivided the Chihuahuan Desert as he did the Sonoran. In 1945 he wrote:

> In spite of floristic differences, there is a strong similarity between comparable situations in the northern and southern parts of the desert. . . .
>
> There are no parts of the Chihuahuan Desert in which the ground is as thickly covered with diversified groups of striking plants as in many localities in Sonora and Baja California. Only in Zacatecas and San Luis Potosi does the occurrence of tall yuccas, *Acacia Farnesiana*, and large platyopuntias and agaves give striking evidence of the somewhat ameliorated conditions which exist along the southern edge of the Chihuahuan Desert.[7]

Aside from reports in the *Carnegie Yearbook*, Shreve's first paper on the Chihuahuan Desert was also his last. With World War II came gasoline rationing, which retarded the progress of the project between 1942 and 1944. Shreve was too old to serve in the military, but Johnston worked as a research consultant to the Chemical Warfare Service in Panama. By the time the war ended, Shreve had retired, and his deteriorating health combined with lack of funding made field trips impracticable. In his last report in the *Carnegie Yearbook* in 1945, Shreve anticipated the completion of the project within the next two years, but when he died five years later, it was still unfinished.

When Shreve retired in 1945, he did not retire from the Desert Laboratory. It no longer existed. The Carnegie Institution had closed it in 1940, after thirty-seven years of desert research.

As early as 1934 Merriam had seriously considered closing the laboratory. In a memo to Spoehr, Merriam had written, "The fact [is] that the expense is too large for the Desert Laboratory as a field station. Shreve's work is good but it is doubtful if the laboratory is necessary to support it. Shreve himself does not seem able to measure up to a vigorous program." Looking to the future, Merriam decided it would "be necessary to make change[s] which will either eliminate the Desert Laboratory or reduce the staff and expense, or discover means which are of outstanding importance by which the Desert Laboratory can be put in the field of institutions doing work of the highest rank."[8]

All through the thirties there were signs that the laboratory was becoming increasingly dispensable in the eyes of Carnegie Institution administrators. The first indication was Shreve's difficulty in organizing a celebration for the thirtieth anniversary of the laboratory in 1933. Starting in 1929 he laid plans for the occasion. He invited the scientists who had worked at the laboratory over the years to prepare papers reviewing their studies there. In August 1933 he reminded Spoehr that the celebration was only a few months away. "I hope very much that you will be able to come down for this and will be prepared to make a short talk on the possibilities for work in such a Laboratory," Shreve said.[9] Spoehr declined with the excuse that "under present circumstances such an undertaking could be justified only on the basis of the direct scientific contributions which may result."[10] In the end Shreve, MacDougal, Thornber, Mallery, and a few others lunched at the Old Pueblo Club on October 7 to mark the occasion.

Signs of the impending collapse accumulated. Shreve had hoped to keep Robert Humphrey for an extra year, but the necessary funds were not available. Then, in 1936, Spoehr tried to eliminate Mallery's job. In an angry and anguished response, Shreve wrote, "Your intimations that Mallery is out of the picture come as a bitter shock."[11] He insisted that Mallery was the one person who made fieldwork possible. Perhaps swayed by Shreve's uncharacteristically emotional reply, Spoehr made no further moves to eliminate Mallery, who remained at the Desert Laboratory a few more years. If Shreve retained existing staff with difficulty, he found it impossible to hire new staff. "Nothing would suit me better than to have about four men here to take up some of the many things that need to be done along physiological lines as well as in ecology, histology, and anatomy," he said in 1936.[12] But the opportunity for expansion never arrived.

Carnegie funds were heavily dependent on railway stocks, which had lost value during the depression. To compensate, the institution needed to cut expenses, so it closed the Desert Laboratory, Clements's Alpine Laboratory, the Marine Biology Laboratory at Dry Tortugas, and several other research stations. (Spoehr's laboratory remained open.) Perhaps if Shreve had been a better politician he could have forestalled the administrators. Although Merriam and others at the Carnegie Institution liked him personally and respected him as a scientist, Shreve could not, it seems, convey the importance of his work. Spoehr summarized this basic problem when he told Shreve that the institution's trustees at times felt "that some of the work is not of a very serious nature, that much of the exploration and expedition work is a bit of glorified camping and vacationing. To the factual mind, it is difficult to understand what this type of work is contributing to the body of knowledge."[13] MacDougal had clashed with Woodward two decades earlier for the same reasons. It seems likely that Spoehr, perhaps unwittingly, characterized his own attitude toward Shreve's research in those remarks.

In part the gulf between Shreve and Spoehr was that between the experimentalist and the observer. Spoehr was a laboratory scientist whose data came from experiments conducted under controlled conditions. Shreve was a field scientist whose data came from observations made over a wide range of natural conditions. As an experimentalist, Spoehr might have doubted the elegance of Shreve's methods and therefore the value of his results. Spoehr would have found ample encouragement for his position in the goals and structure of the Carnegie Institution, which was becoming increasingly oriented toward experimental work and high technology.

Merriam, a paleontologist, might have felt more sympathy for observational methods but even so showed little understanding of

The Desert Laboratory staff about 1938: left to right, *Arthur Hinckley, Forrest Shreve, Edith Shreve, Howard Scott Gentry, T. D. Mallery, and William Turnage*

the nature and scope of Shreve's work. Merriam complained that the laboratory's research program lacked vision and vigor but at the same time refused to provide the financial support needed for a more visionary program.

Had the necessary funds been available, Shreve might well have developed the Sonoran Desert project into a precursor of ecosystem ecology. As early as 1934, he had suggested that a multidisciplinary approach involving climatologists, geologists, botanists, zoologists, and others was the best way to study the desert, just as scientists from a variety of fields drew together to study the ocean. Yet although he knew of "a score of oceanographic institutions and over two hundred marine and fresh-water laboratories," he could list only "three small laboratories in the world in which the scientific problems of the desert are being pursued."[14]

Those who knew Shreve well in the thirties have remarked that the only time they saw him depressed was when the laboratory was shut down. The closing of the Desert Laboratory was a particularly cruel blow for Shreve because he had seen himself not as a superstar scientist but as part of a team of dedicated researchers. If there was a superstar in his mind, it was the Desert Laboratory itself, its mission and everything it stood for. He attempted to interest the University of Arizona in taking it over; at least that way, its original mission would continue to be fulfilled. The university could have bought the laboratory buildings and grounds for one dollar but decided not to because of maintenance costs. (It eventually purchased the facility in 1960 for $140,500.) In 1940 the Forest Service took over the buildings and grounds. Shreve was given office space to use until he retired, and the Carnegie Institution continued to fund him at a lower level until 1945, making it possible for him to visit the Chihuahuan Desert three times in the forties.

Vannevar Bush, the new president of the Carnegie Institution, wrote in 1940 that in closing the Desert Laboratory the institution had "succeeded in avoiding the sacrifice of valuable elements." Bush noted that the kind of work done at the laboratory was now "incorporated into the large operations of the government in connection with forestry, soil conservation, and the public domain." Therefore, the institution had "transferred the property at Tucson to the Forest Service for use in its research program, which has objectives closely parallel to those which prompted the early establishment of this laboratory."[15] In retrospect, his statement seems disingenuous. The goals of the Forest Service were not, as it turned out, in sympathy with those of the Desert Laboratory. During their twenty-year tenure of Tumamoc Hill, Forest Service officials allowed much unnecessary and irreparable destruction of native vegetation on the grounds.

Although the Carnegie Institution had no money for Shreve's lab, nor for Clements's, there was enough money for the Department of Terrestrial Magnetism to build a cyclotron and for the institution to cooperate with the California Institute of Technology in constructing a two-hundred-inch telescope. Basically, the Carnegie Institution was no longer sympathetic to ecological research. Even had Shreve been a consummate politician, he could not have changed his field attire for a lab coat; he could not have danced to the experimentalists' tune.

After the laboratory closed, Shreve completed several projects he had begun in the late thirties, including a summary of rainfall data from forty-four weather stations in northern Mexico, a chapter on the vegetation of Arizona for Thomas H. Kearney and Robert H. Peebles's *Flowering Plants and Ferns of Arizona*, and a description of the grasslands of northern Mexico. His most important work from this period was a long paper describing the vegetation of the four North American deserts.

Since its publication in 1942, "The Desert Vegetation of North America" has become the standard work on the subject, largely because ecologists, geographers, and others frequently cite Shreve's map of the Great Basin, Mojave, Sonoran, and Chihuahuan deserts. Shreve emphasized that the sharp boundaries he drew on the map did not exist in nature: rather, the severe conditions in the interior of the desert gradually ameliorated toward its edges, so that drawing desert boundaries was largely a matter of trying to "connect the localities which exhibit the same stages of transition from arid to semi-arid vegetation."[16]

Shreve took an observational, descriptive approach to delineating the four deserts. He said, "In the study of any body of vegetation three fundamental questions arise: What kinds of plants does it contain? How are they associated? What is their taxonomic position?" Adequate answers to these questions, Shreve wrote, "will give a complete characterization of the vegetation, and will make it then possible to determine its geographical range, its habitat location, its successional relations, and its controlling physiological conditions."[17]

Shreve intended to study in detail all the deserts of North America, but as he told plant collector Percy Train in 1937, their area "is so large that we are compelled to attack it a little at a time." After the "long program of work in the Mexican deserts of the west coast and the Central Plateau" is finished, he said, he hoped "to do more than we have yet done with the Mohave Desert and finally to study the plains of Utah and Nevada."[18] Had he remained healthy and had the Desert Laboratory stayed open, he might have realized these plans. But the long paper on desert vegetation was the closest he came.

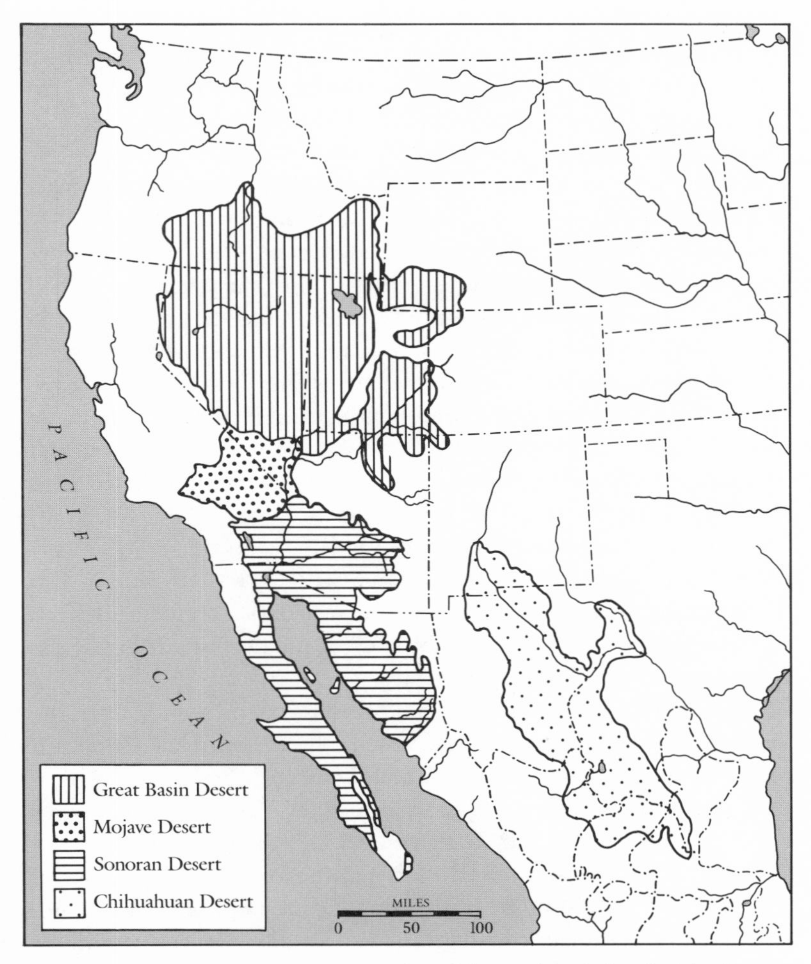

Four major deserts of North America first delineated and described by Forrest Shreve (after Shreve 1942)

In 1950 Shreve was appointed honorary president of the Seventh International Botanical Congress, one of the highest distinctions a botanist can receive. He was too modest to record the event in his diary, but he did save the parchment announcement. His uncertain health prevented him from attending the congress.

During the last thirteen years of his life, Shreve found himself limited more and more by poor health. In January 1937 a laboratory vessel containing sulphuric acid exploded in his face. He was rather badly burned, and the immediate effects of the injury were intensified because the pipes in the laboratory were frozen. Edith used distilled water and ammonia to bathe his face and eyes, and he suffered no permanent injury other than scarring on his face. In subsequent years, Shreve was troubled by recurrent prostate infections, a duodenal ulcer, back pain, arthritis, persistent dizziness, heart disease, and frequent colds and flu. His weight occasionally dropped as low as 120 pounds, hardly sufficient for a man more than six feet tall. Although his official retirement date was July 1, 1945, his days at the office dwindled after 1941, and he had essentially retired by 1943. His weak heart was characteristic of patients who had at one time suffered from rheumatic fever, and when he died, his doctor attributed the cause of death to an enlarged heart.

By the time of Shreve's final illness, most of his friends from the Desert Laboratory days had dispersed. MacDougal, who outlived Shreve by eight years, was in Carmel. Duncan Johnson had died in 1937, Hinckley in 1943, Livingston in 1948. Mallery was abroad with the Foreign Service, and Turnage had left in 1939. Gentry, who dropped in occasionally after the laboratory closed, was out of town.

Edith was with him, however, when he died at home on July 19, 1950. The last entry in his diary is for that day: written in Edith's hand are the words "Forrest Shreve died."

Weaving the Threads

During the decades since Shreve's death, some of his research topics have become important concepts in plant ecology: aridity is a stimulus to plant evolution; distribution of a plant species reflects its tolerance for a range of environmental conditions, thus few if any species have identical distributions; trends in establishment and mortality in plant populations tell much about the conditions necessary for growth; changes in climate and vegetation along an environmental gradient reveal the conditions that limit a plant's distribution.[1]

Shreve's relatively slight influence during his lifetime was due in part to Clementsian ecology and in part to his own attitudes and interests. He was essentially an innovative researcher in a particular place, and his interests were the ecological problems that place presented. For much of Shreve's life, his place was the desert, especially the Sonoran Desert.

When Shreve came to Tucson at the age of twenty-nine, he was determined to be an ecologist but was not necessarily committed to a lifetime in the desert. The problems, rather than the place, aroused his enthusiasm at first; in fact, his early impression of the desert was of a harsh and uninviting place. He later recalled that, when he arrived at the Desert Laboratory in June 1908,

> the spring had been a very dry one and the vegetation was at a low ebb. The physical elements of the desert, however, were at the highest level of their intensity: the temperature high, the humidity low, the sunshine brilliant, the wind incessant and variable, raising towers of dust which slowly moved across the broad Santa Cruz Valley, whirling continually with majestic grace. To one whose previous experience had all been in the eastern states and the humid uplands of Jamaica, the aspect of the desert was deeply impressive. It seemed incredible that the creosote bushes, with only a few dark brown leaves, were really alive. It was a mystery that the mesquite and acacia were able to flaunt their leaves to the air without the loss of more water than the hopelessly dry soil could furnish them. A score of featureless gray shrubs were barren of anything that indicated their relationship. Even the cacti were drooping and yellowing.[2]

But with the first heavy summer rains a week or two later, the renewal of desert life gave him hope. Here was no half-dead ecosystem but one burgeoning with life and possibilities. In later years he described his first desert thunderstorm:

> Shortly after our return from the mountains, great cumulus clouds began to fill the sky every afternoon. After a week of this performance, late one afternoon the snowy clouds suddenly blackened, lightning began a continuous fusillade and rain poured down for nearly an hour. The coming of the first heavy rain of summer is the most important biological episode of the year. At a single stroke the country is transformed from desert to tropics. . . . The awakening of dormant animal life is a matter of only a few hours. The quickening of plant activity is manifest within 48 hours. Flowers burst forth from shrubs on which buds were scarcely discernible a few days before. New shoots and new leaves develop rapidly on the trees and shrubs. . . . Myriads of seedlings appear and develop so rapidly that many of them can be identified by an experienced observer in 40 to 60 hours after the activating rain.[3]

When Shreve moved to the desert from Maryland, he brought the biases of a person who had always lived in a humid climate. He believed that his new home was an inhospitable environment for plants and animals and only slowly came to realize that their adaptations made the desert as favorable for them as Maryland's climate was for hickory trees and raccoons. The study of the desert became for Shreve not the study of an inimical environment but the study of life under extreme physical conditions.

With his transformation into a desert ecologist came a broadening of his interest from vegetation to the entire ecosystem. He came to understand that a holistic approach to desert research would be the most fruitful. "We need to weave together the separate threads of knowledge about the plants and their natural setting into a close fabric of understanding in which it will be possible to see the whole pattern and design of desert life."[4]

Shreve eventually came to believe that "the most significant lesson that the desert dweller can learn from a familiarity with its plant and animal life is to regard himself not as an exile from some better place but as a man at home in an environment to which his life can be adjusted without physical or intellectual loss."[5] His friends understood that this statement embodied the essence of his life. C. H. Muller, plant ecologist and taxonomist, said, "When I first met Shreve I found him to be a man intellectually in tune with the desert landscape and its people. As I became more intimately acquainted with him, this impression grew."[6] Robert Humphrey and Ira Wiggins wrote that Shreve "became almost a part of the desert he studied and knew so well."[7] Howard Scott Gentry paid the finest tribute of all when he said that Shreve "was desertic in his patience and his detachment, and like the desert, he put on a good display when he flowered."[8]

Appendix

Common Plant Names and Their Scientific Equivalents

acacia	*Acacia constricta* Benth.
barrel cactus	*Ferocactus* spp.
big galleta	*Hilaria rigida* (Thurb.) Benth.
big sagebrush	*Artemisia tridentata* Nutt.
blue palo verde	*Cercidium floridum* Benth.
boojum tree	*Idria columnaris* Kell.
brittlebush	*Encelia farinosa* Gray
bursage	*Ambrosia* spp.
cardón	*Pachycereus pringlei* (S. Wats.) Britt. & Rose
catclaw	*Acacia greggii* Gray
century plant	*Agave shawii* Engelm.
cholla	*Opuntia versicolor* Engelm.
cirio	*Idria columnaris* Kell.
coldenia	*Tiquilia canescens* (DC.) A. Richardson
columbine	*Aquilegia chrysantha* Gray
creosote bush	*Larrea tridentata* (DC.) Cov.
desert holly	*Atriplex hymenelytra* (Torr.) Wats.
elephant tree	*Bursera microphylla* Gray
fairy duster	*Calliandra eriophylla* Benth.
fig-wort	*Scrophularia parviflora* Woot. & Standl.
hemlock	*Tsuga canadensis* (L.) Carr.

ironwood	*Olneya tesota* Gray
Joshua tree	*Yucca brevifolia* Engelm.
juniper	*Juniperus* spp.
limber bush	*Jatropha cinerea* (Ort.) Muell.-Arg.
little-leaf palo verde	*Cercidium microphyllum* (Torr.) Rose & Johnst.
magnolia	*Magnolia* spp.
manzanita	*Arctostaphylos* spp.
mesquite	*Prosopis* spp.
Mormon tea	*Ephedra* spp.
oak	*Quercus* spp.
ocotillo	*Fouquieria splendens* Engelm.
organ pipe cactus	*Lemaireocereus thurberi* (Engelm.) Britt. & Rose
palo verde	*Cercidium* spp.
pincushion cactus	*Mammillaria* spp.
pine	*Pinus* spp.
pitcher plant	*Sarracenia purpurea* L.
prickly pear	*Opuntia* spp.
redwood	*Sequoia sempervirens* (Lamb.) Endl.
rudbeckia	*Rudbeckia laciniata* L.
saguaro	*Carnegiea gigantea* Engelm.
senita	*Lophocereus schottii* (Engelm.) Britt. & Rose
torchwood	*Bursera hindsiana* (Benth.) Engler
tree ocotillo	*Fouquieria macdougalii* Nash
triangle-leaf bursage	*Ambrosia deltoidea* (Torr.) Payne
tulip tree	*Liriodendron tulipifera* L.
velvet mesquite	*Prosopis velutina* Woot.
white bursage	*Ambrosia dumosa* (Gray) Payne
yucca	*Yucca valida* Brandegee

Notes to the Chapters

Abbreviations

AHC	Arizona Heritage Center, Arizona Historical Society
CIW	Carnegie Institution of Washington
SC	Special Collections, University of Arizona Library
UAH	University of Arizona Herbarium

Preface

1. F. Shreve, "Plant life of the Sonoran Desert," *Scientific Monthly* 42 (1936): 213.

His Home the Desert

1. F. S. Shreve, "The plant resources of the Southwest" (1926), 12. Unpublished manuscript, SC.
2. Ibid., 11.
3. Ibid., 14.
4. R. P. McIntosh, "Ecology since 1900," in B. J. Taylor and T. J. White, eds., *Issues and Ideas in America* (Norman: University of Oklahoma Press, 1976), 354.
5. R. P. McIntosh, "Pioneer support for ecology," *BioScience* 33 (1983): 107–12.

6. See, for example, W. D. Billings, "American deserts and their mountains: An ecological frontier," *Bulletin of the Ecological Society of America* 61 (1980): 203–9. Also see R. H. Whittaker, "Classification of communities," *Botanical Review* 28 (1962): 1–239.

7. Quoted in F. B. Tolles, *Meeting House and Counting House: The Quaker Merchants of Colonial Philadelphia, 1682–1763* (Chapel Hill: University of North Carolina Press, 1948), 211.

8. F. Shreve to R. Pyle, 19 June 1931, SC.

9. A. S. Eddington, *Science and the Unseen World* (New York: Macmillan, 1929). F. B. Tolles also noted the affinity of Quakers for science in *Quakers and the Atlantic Culture* (New York: Macmillan, 1960).

10. J. Bowden, *The History of the Society of Friends in America*, vol. 1 (London: Charles Gilpin, 1850; New York: Arno Press, 1972).

11. R. C. Tobey, in *Saving the Prairies* (Berkeley: University of California Press, 1981), notes that at the University of Nebraska, a land-grant college, biologists focused on technical problems of grassland agriculture, whereas at the University of Chicago, a private school, they concentrated on pure science. He points out that Frederic Clements, a Nebraska graduate, often tackled applied problems, but Chicago graduate Henry C. Cowles, like Shreve, was more interested in theoretical matters.

12. F. Shreve to D. Johnson, 11 March 1931, SC.

13. F. Shreve to W. S. Cooper, 23 Oct. 1930, SC.

14. McIntosh, "Ecology since 1900," 354.

15. F. E. Egler, "Forrest Shreve and the Sonoran Desert," *The Geographical Review* 44 (1954): 137–41.

Getting Experience

1. At the time of the Maryland Botanical Survey, F. H. Blodgett was an assistant plant pathologist for the state of Maryland; F. W. Besley was a state forester; and M. A. Chrysler was an assistant botanist for the survey. None of these men developed careers in ecology.

2. F. Shreve et al., *The Plant Life of Maryland* (Baltimore: Johns Hopkins University Press, 1910), 24.

3. Quoted in R. P. McIntosh, "Ecology since 1900," 355.

4. The early history of physiological ecology has been discussed by W. D. Billings in "American deserts and their mountains" and by R. P. McIntosh in "Ecology since 1900."

5. A. F. W. Schimper, *Plant-Geography Upon a Physiological Basis* (Oxford: Clarendon Press, 1903), iv. R. J. Goodland, in "The tropical origin of ecology: Eugen Warming's jubilee," *Oikos* 26 (1975): 240–45, has argued that Schimper plagiarized Warming's data and results.

6. F. V. Coville et al., *Carnegie Yearbook*, vol. 1, 1902 (Washington, D. C.: Carnegie Institution of Washington, 1903), 5. Historical accounts of the founding of the Desert Laboratory can be found in W. G. McGinnies, *Discovering the Desert* (Tucson: University of Arizona Press, 1981); J. C. Wilder, "The years of a desert laboratory," *Journal of Arizona History* 8 (1967): 179–99; and R. P. McIntosh, "Pioneer support for ecology."

7. R. P. McIntosh, in "Pioneer support for ecology," discusses in more detail the effect of the new Desert Laboratory on the developing field of ecology.

8. MacDougal had evidently formed a high opinion of Shreve's Jamaican work. While in Jamaica in 1905 and 1906, Shreve had cultivated certain experimental plants for MacDougal and made evaporation measurements for Burton Livingston.

9. F. Shreve to D. T. MacDougal, 15 April 1907, AHC.

10. D. T. MacDougal to N. L. Britton, 26 July 1907, AHC.

A Good Fit All Around

1. M. S. Conn to W. G. McGinnies, 23 Aug. 1973.

2. J. R. Brown, *Adventures in the Apache Country: A Tour Through Arizona and Sonora, 1864* (Tucson: University of Arizona Press, 1974), 22.

3. H. S. Reed, "Volney Morgan Spalding," *Plant World* 22 (1918): 15.

4. V. M. Spalding to D. T. MacDougal, 29 June 1907, AHC.

5. V. M. Spalding to D. T. MacDougal, 1 Aug. 1907, AHC.

6. H. A. Gleason to C. H. Muller, 18 Feb. 1952. Published as "Delving into the history of American ecology," *Bulletin of the Ecological Society of America* 56 (1975): 8.

7. D. T. MacDougal, *Carnegie Yearbook*, vol. 5, 1906 (Washington, D. C.: Carnegie Institution of Washington, 1907), 21. The results of the acclimatization work were published in D. T. MacDougal, "The reactions of plants to new habitats," *Ecology* 2 (1921): 1–20.

8. D. T. MacDougal to N. L. Britton, 17 Oct. 1908, AHC.

The Limbo of Controversy

1. F. Shreve to D. T. MacDougal, 2 July 1909, AHC.

2. F. Shreve to D. T. MacDougal, 6 Sept. 1909, AHC.

3. Ibid.

4. F. Shreve, *A Montane Rain-Forest: A Contribution to the Physiological Plant Geography of Jamaica*, Carnegie Institution of Washington Publication no. 199 (Washington, D. C., 1914), 59.

5. Ibid., 86.

6. Ibid., 59.

7. F. Shreve, "The direct effects of rainfall on hygrophilous vegetation," *Journal of Ecology* 2 (1914): 91. J. M. Dean and A. P. Smith in "Behavioral and morphological adaptations of a tropical plant to high rainfall," *Biotropica* 10 (1978): 152–54, have demonstrated that drip-tips of *Machaerium arborium*, a Panamanian leguminous liana, do indeed hasten drying of the leaf surface. They suggest that Shreve worked with plants that had abbreviated, atypical drip-tips, thus his negative results.

8. S. J. Gould and R. C. Lewontin, "The spandrels of San Marco and the Panglossian paradigm: A critique of the adaptationist programme," *Proceedings of the Royal Society of London* B 205 (1979): 581–98.

9. Ibid., 587.

10. D. S. Johnson, "A montane rain forest," *Science* 40 (1914): 897.

11. Shreve, *Montane Rain-Forest*, 28.

12. Ibid., 28–29.

13. Ibid., 32.

14. Ibid., 33.

15. Ibid., 107.

16. Ibid., 106.

17. Ibid., 110.

18. G. D. Fuller, "A montane rain-forest," *Botanical Gazette* 60 (1915): 239.

19. F. Shreve to D. T. MacDougal, 6 Sept. 1909, AHC.

Energy, Push, and Solid Horse Sense

1. E. N. Transeau to D. T. MacDougal, 23 Feb. 1910, AHC.

2. D. T. MacDougal to E. N. Transeau, 28 Feb. 1910, AHC.

3. B. E. Livingston to D. T. MacDougal, 20 Aug. 1910, AHC.

4. B. E. Livingston to D. T. MacDougal, 26 Aug. 1911, AHC.

5. F. Shreve to D. T. MacDougal, 12 Dec. 1912, AHC.

6. Ibid.

7. D. T. MacDougal to F. Shreve, 20 Dec. 1912, AHC.

8. In 1914 the Botanical Society of America established its own journal, *The American Journal of Botany*. F. C. Newcombe was its first editor.

9. F. Shreve to D. T. MacDougal, 6 Sept. 1909, AHC.

10. J. L. Harper, "A Darwinian approach to plant ecology," *Journal of Ecology* 55 (1967): 247. Shreve had undoubtedly read Darwin's *Origin of Species*, but it seems likely that Shreve's ideas about plant population biology were independently derived.

11. R. M. Turner, U. S. Geological Survey, has been monitoring saguaro populations on Tumamoc Hill, where they have made a striking comeback since Shreve's time. East of Tucson, however, W. F. Steenbergh and C. H. Lowe have documented a dramatic decrease in saguaro numbers at the Rincon Mountain Unit of Saguaro National Monument. See W. F. Steenbergh and C. H. Lowe, *Ecology of the Saguaro: II. Reproduction, Germination, Establishment, Growth, and Survival of the Young Plant*, National Park Service Scientific Monograph Series no. 8. (Washington, D. C., 1977); and W. F. Steenbergh and C. H. Lowe, *Ecology of the Saguaro: III. Growth and Demography*, National Park Service Scientific Monograph Series no. 17 (Washington, D.C., 1983).

12. F. Shreve, "Establishment behavior of the palo verde," *Plant World* 14 (1911): 296.

13. P. J. Grubb, "The maintenance of species-richness in plant communities: The importance of the regeneration niche," *Biological Review* 52 (1977): 133.

14. F. Shreve, "The establishment of desert perennials," *Journal of Ecology* 5 (1917): 216.

15. L. O. Sheps, "Survival of *Larrea tridentata* seedlings in Death Valley National Monument, California," *Israel Journal of Botany* 22 (1973): 8–17.

16. R. S. Boyd and G. D. Brum, "Post-dispersal reproductive biology of a Mojave Desert population of *Larrea tridentata* (Zygophyllaceae)," *American Midland Naturalist* 110 (1983): 25–36.

17. J. R. McAuliffe, "Herbivore-limited establishment of a Sonoran Desert tree, *Cercidium microphyllum*," *Ecology* 67 (1986): 276–80.

18. F. Shreve, "Cold air drainage," *Plant World* 15 (1912): 115.

19. F. Shreve, "Rainfall as a determinant of soil moisture," *Plant World* 17 (1914): 9.

20. Ibid., 21.

21. F. Shreve, "The influence of low temperature on the distribution of giant cactus," *Plant World* 14 (1911): 143–44.

22. Ibid., 146.

23. F. Shreve, *Carnegie Yearbook*, vol. 10, 1911 (Washington, D. C.: Carnegie Institution of Washington, 1912), 57.

24. For discussions of competition among desert plants, see J. Vandermeer, "Saguaros and nurse trees: A new hypothesis to account for population fluctuations," *Southwestern Naturalist* 25 (1980): 357–60; J. R. McAuliffe, "Sahuaro-nurse tree associations in the Sonoran Desert: competitive effects of sahuaros," *Oecologia* 64 (1984): 319–21; and R. Robberecht, B. E. Mahall, and P. S. Nobel, "Experimental removal of intraspecific competitors—Effects on water relations and productivity of a desert bunchgrass, *Hilaria rigida*," *Oecologia* 60 (1983): 21–24.

25. F. E. Clements, *Plant Succession*, Carnegie Institution of Washington Publication no. 242 (Washington, D. C., 1916), 72.
26. Ibid., 73.
27. Shreve, "Establishment behavior," 290.

Tumamocville

1. D. T. MacDougal to A. M. Vail, 2 May 1913, AHC.
2. D. T. MacDougal to B. E. Livingston, 12 March 1913, AHC.
3. F. Shreve to D. T. MacDougal, 29 June 1915, AHC.
4. D. T. MacDougal to B. E. Livingston, 4 April 1913, AHC.
5. F. Shreve to D. T. MacDougal, 11 July 1913, AHC.
6. D. T. MacDougal to R. B. von Kleinsmid, 1914, AHC.
7. F. Shreve to D. T. MacDougal, 24 Aug. 1912, AHC.
8. F. Shreve to D. T. MacDougal, 11 July 1913, AHC.
9. D. T. MacDougal to H. S. Gale, 23 Aug. 1912, AHC.
10. G. Sykes, *A Westerly Trend* (Tucson: Arizona Pioneers Historical Society, 1944), 275–76. Reprinted by the University of Arizona Press, 1985.
11. T. H. Kearney and R. H. Peebles, *Flowering Plants and Ferns of Arizona*, USDA Miscellaneous Publication no. 423 (Washington, D. C., 1942). J. E. Bowers, "The making of a flora for Arizona, 1901–1951," *Desert Plants* 7 (1985): 181–83, 211, tells how *Flowering Plants and Ferns* came to be written.
12. F. Shreve to D. T. MacDougal, 15 July 1915, AHC.
13. F. Shreve to D. T. MacDougal, 22 Aug. 1914, AHC.
14. F. Shreve to D. T. MacDougal, 28 July 1916, AHC.
15. F. Shreve to D. T. MacDougal, 16 Nov. 1917, AHC.

The Shifting Panorama

1. Shreve, "Ecological work," 15–16, SC.
2. D. T. MacDougal to B. E. Livingston, 28 Oct. 1910, AHC.
3. D. T. MacDougal to B. E. Livingston, 31 March 1910, AHC.
4. D. T. MacDougal to G. Sykes, 27 July 1908, AHC.
5. F. Shreve to D. T. MacDougal, 27 Oct. 1914, AHC.
6. D. T. MacDougal to R. S. Woodward, 20 March 1915, AHC.
7. R. H. Whittaker and W. A. Niering, "Vegetation of the Santa Catalina Mountains, Arizona: A gradient analysis of the south slope," *Ecology* 46 (1965): 432.
8. F. Shreve, *Carnegie Yearbook*, vol. 14, 1915 (Washington, D. C.: Carnegie Institution of Washington, 1916), 84–85.
9. F. Shreve, *Vegetation of a Desert Mountain Range as Conditioned by*

Climatic Factors, Carnegie Institution of Washington Publication no. 217 (Washington, D. C., 1915), 6.

10. Ibid., 13.
11. Ibid., 11.
12. Ibid., 15
13. Ibid., 112.
14. Ibid., 58.
15. Ibid., 101.
16. Ibid., 104.
17. Ibid., 107.
18. Ibid., 100.
19. Ibid.
20. Ibid., 111–12.
21. D. T. MacDougal to R. S. Woodward, 19 Aug. 1915, SC.
22. D. T. MacDougal to F. Shreve, 29 June 1915, AHC.
23. F. Shreve to D. T. MacDougal, 1 July 1915, AHC.

Point and Counterpoint

1. D. T. MacDougal to R. S. Woodward, 8 May 1913, AHC; D. T. MacDougal to N. L. Britton, 31 March 1914, AHC.
2. Clements, *Plant Succession*, 125.
3. Ibid., 124–25.
4. A. G. Tansley, "Frederic Edward Clements," *Journal of Ecology* 34 (1947): 194.
5. Tobey, *Saving the Prairies*, 76.
6. F. E. Egler, "A commentary on American plant ecology, based on the textbooks of 1947–1949," *Ecology* 32 (1951): 677.
7. Ibid., 678.
8. R. H. Whittaker, "A criticism of the plant association and climatic climax concepts," *Northwest Science* 25 (1951): 28. Certain ecologists have revived Clementsian ideas of succession, among them J. A. MacMahon, "Ecosystems over time: Succession and other types of change," in R. H. Waring, ed., *Forests: Fresh Perspectives from Ecosystem Analysis* (Corvallis: Oregon State University Press, 1980), 27–58.
9. Egler, "American plant ecology," 678.
10. F. E. Clements to D. T. MacDougal, 16 April 1907, AHC.
11. Clements, *Plant Succession*, iii.
12. B. E. Livingston to D. T. MacDougal, 26 Jan. 1918, AHC.
13. Tansley, "Frederic Edward Clements," 196.
14. C. H. Muller, "Resolution of respect, Henry Allan Gleason, 1882–1975," *Bulletin of the Ecological Society of America* 56 (1975): 25.

15. "Dr. H. A. Gleason, Distinguished Ecologist," *Bulletin of the Ecological Society of America* 34 (1953): 41.

16. Shreve, *Vegetation of a Desert Mountain Range*, 111.

17. S. A. Cain, "Henry Allan Gleason, Eminent Ecologist 1959," *Bulletin of the Ecological Society of America* 40 (1959): 105–10.

18. Muller, "Resolution of respect," 25.

19. This discussion of Gleason's life and work is based on R. P. McIntosh, "H. A. Gleason—'Individualistic Ecologist' 1882–1975: His contributions to ecological theory," *Bulletin of the Torrey Botanical Club* 102 (1975): 253–73. The continuum concept was revived in 1947. C. H. Lowe, "Biotic communities in the sub-Mogollon region of the inland Southwest," *Journal of the Arizona Academy of Science* 2 (1961): 40–49, was evidently the first to recognize Shreve's priority in the matter. W. D. Billings, in "American deserts and their mountains," independently arrived at the same conclusion in 1980.

20. F. Shreve to P. C. Standley, 23 Sept. 1930, SC.

Mountain Islands

1. F. Shreve to D. T. MacDougal, 29 July 1914, AHC.

2. Shreve, *Vegetation of a Desert Mountain Range*, 39.

3. Ibid., 41.

4. Ibid., 40.

5. Ibid., 40–41.

6. F. Shreve, "A comparison of the vegetational features of two desert mountain ranges," *Plant World* 22 (1919): 305.

7. F. Shreve, *Carnegie Yearbook*, vol. 14, 1915 (Washington, D. C.: Carnegie Institution of Washington, 1916), 87.

8. F. Shreve, *Carnegie Yearbook*, vol. 16, 1917 (Washington, D. C.: Carnegie Institution of Washington, 1918), 93.

9. Shreve, "A comparison of the vegetational features," 306.

10. Ibid.

11. Explanations of Pleistocene plant movements have been summarized by P. S. Martin in *The Last 10,000 Years* (Tucson: University of Arizona Press, 1963) and by T. R. Van Devender and W. G. Spaulding in "Development of vegetation and climate in the southwestern United States," *Science* 204 (1979): 701–10. In *The Theory of Island Biogeography* (Princeton University Press, 1967), Robert H. MacArthur and Edward O. Wilson mathematically model immigration and extinction rates for insular biotas. Kimball T. Harper, among others, has applied island biogeography to southwestern mountain ranges; see K. T. Harper et al., "The flora of Great Basin mountain ranges: Diversity, sources, and dispersal ecology," *Great Basin Naturalist Memoirs* 2 (1978): 81–103.

12. F. Shreve to D. T. MacDougal, 29 June 1915, AHC.

Our Mutual Arbeit

1. D. T. MacDougal to G. A. Mower, 2 Dec. 1914, AHC.
2. F. Shreve to D. T. MacDougal, 20 July 1917, AHC.
3. Ibid.
4. D. T. MacDougal to E. E. Free, 4 May 1915, AHC.
5. R. S. Woodward to D. T. MacDougal, 16 Nov. 1915, AHC.
6. F. Shreve to D. T. MacDougal, 16 Jan. 1915, AHC.
7. F. Shreve to D. T. MacDougal, 28 March 1916, AHC.
8. B. E. Livingston to D. T. MacDougal, 4 June 1908, AHC.
9. C. H. Merriam, "Laws of temperature control of the geographic distribution of terrestrial plants and animals," *National Geographic Magazine* 6 (1894): 229.
10. E. N. Transeau, "Climatic centers and centers of plant distribution," *Annual Report of the Michigan Academy of Science* 7 (1905): 73.
11. E. N. Transeau, "Forest centers of eastern North America," *American Naturalist* 39 (1905): 875–89.
12. F. Shreve, "Excursion impressions," *Transactions of the San Diego Society of Natural History* 2 (1916): 82.
13. Ibid.
14. B. E. Livingston to D. T. MacDougal, 20 May 1910, AHC.
15. B. E. Livingston to D. T. MacDougal, 24 Sept. 1914, AHC.
16. D. B. Lawrence, "Introduction," *Ecology* 29 (1948): 228.
17. Ibid., 227.
18. B. E. Livingston to D. T. MacDougal, 20 March 1913, AHC.
19. Gleason's statement ("Delving into the history," 7) that Shreve was a student of Livingston's is incorrect.
20. D. T. MacDougal to H. M. Richards, 20 Sept. 1915, AHC.
21. F. Shreve to D. T. MacDougal, 25 Feb. 1916, AHC.
22. B. E. Livingston to D. T. MacDougal, 20 April 1916, AHC.
23. F. Shreve to D. T. MacDougal, 9 Aug. 1917, AHC.
24. Oddly, this treatment diverged from the classification scheme Livingston and Shreve eventually presented in *The Distribution of Vegetation in the United States*. On pages 22–23, they recommended a hierarchical scheme of formation, association, and society, similar in some respects to Clements's system. It seems likely that Livingston suggested this scheme; at any rate, Shreve never used it in subsequent publications.
25. B. E. Livingston and F. Shreve, *The Distribution of Vegetation in the United States as Related to Climatic Conditions*, Carnegie Institution of Washington Publication no. 284 (Washington, D. C., 1921), 27.
26. Ibid., 25.
27. F. Shreve, *Carnegie Yearbook*, vol. 15, 1916 (Washington, D. C.: Carnegie Institution of Washington, 1917), 72–73.

28. D. T. MacDougal, reporting for B. E. Livingston and F. Shreve, *Carnegie Yearbook*, vol. 7, 1908 (Washington, D.C.: Carnegie Institution of Washington, 1909), 60.

29. Livingston and Shreve, *Distribution of Vegetation*, 3.

30. Ibid., 389.

31. F. Shreve, "What is a desert?" Unpublished manuscript (1922), AHC.

32. F. Shreve, "The edge of the desert," *Yearbook of the Association of Pacific Coast Geographers* 6 (1940): 6–11.

33. B. E. Livingston, "A study of the relation between summer evaporation intensity and centers of plant distribution in the United States," *Plant World* 14 (1911): 216.

34. J. Parker, "Cold resistance in woody plants," *Botanical Review* 29 (1963): 126. Livingston himself was never entirely satisfied with the book, partly because the only evaporation data available were those they had collected during 1908. Many years after publication, Livingston proposed that they collect more data and repeat their calculations, but by then Shreve was busy with other projects and nothing came of the suggestion.

35. Egler, "Forrest Shreve and the Sonoran Desert," 137. Gleason ("Delving into the history," 7) assessed the joint work in the following words: "their chief contribution to ecological ideas...was that succession was caused by changes in the rate of evaporation." It is impossible to know whether Gleason wrote these words out of malice, ignorance, or forgetfulness.

A Place in the Sun

1. F. Shreve to D. T. MacDougal, 26 Jan. 1916, AHC.

2. F. Shreve to D. T. MacDougal, 28 March 1916, AHC.

3. Ibid.

4. F. Shreve to D. T. MacDougal, 4 Aug. 1916, AHC.

5. F. Shreve to H. G. Crawford, 16 June 1930, SC.

6. F. Shreve to D. T. MacDougal, 6 Dec. 1917, AHC.

7. F. Shreve to D. T. MacDougal, 25 Sept. 1918, AHC. Shreve himself did not escape the flu epidemic of 1918. In December 1918, while visiting his parents in Maryland, he became seriously ill with influenza, then pneumonia. He was not well enough to return to Tucson until the end of February.

8. D. T. MacDougal to F. Shreve, 20 Jan. 1919, AHC.

9. F. Shreve to D. T. MacDougal, 6 Feb. 1916, AHC.

10. D. T. MacDougal to F. Shreve, 11 Feb. 1916, AHC.

11. F. Shreve to D. T. MacDougal, 6 Feb. 1916, AHC.

12. D. T. MacDougal to B. Moore, 26 Nov. 1919, AHC.

13. D. T. MacDougal to B. E. Livingston, 18 Dec. 1919, AHC.

14. F. Shreve to C. S. Gager, 14 Oct. 1931, SC.

15. R. L. Burgess, "The Ecological Society of America: Historical data and some preliminary analyses," in F. N. Egerton and R. P. McIntosh, eds., *History of American Ecology* (New York: Arno Press, 1977), 1–24.

16. W. C. Steere, *Biological Abstracts/BIOSIS: The First Fifty Years* (New York: Plenum Press, 1976), 27.

17. F. Shreve to D. T. MacDougal, 8 Oct. 1918, AHC.

18. D. T. MacDougal to B. E. Livingston, 11 March 1926, SC.

The Finest Trip

1. D. T. MacDougal to W. A. Cannon, 26 July 1918, AHC.

2. F. Shreve, "The vegetation of a coastal mountain range," *Ecology* 8 (1927): 30.

3. F. Shreve, "The physical conditions of a coastal mountain range," *Ecology* 8 (1927): 414.

4. Ibid., 412.

5. F. Shreve, *Carnegie Yearbook*, vol. 37, 1937/38 (Washington, D. C.: Carnegie Institution of Washington, 1938), 223.

6. F. Shreve, "Ecological aspects of the deserts of California," *Ecology* 6 (1925): 102.

7. Clements, *Plant Indicators*, 167.

8. Ibid., 174.

9. M. M. Karpiscak, in his studies of the Avra Valley northwest of Tucson, and P. V. Wells and R. H. Webb, in separate studies of ghost towns, have detected successional patterns in the desert.

10. F. Shreve, "Plants of the sand," *Carnegie Institution of Washington News Service Bulletin* no. 4 (Washington, D.C., 1937), 91–96.

11. D. T. MacDougal to W. T. Hornaday, 22 Feb. 1911, AHC.

12. F. Shreve to D. T. MacDougal, 28 July 1916, AHC.

13. D. T. MacDougal to J. W. Harding, 8 May 1925, SC.

14. D. T. MacDougal to N. L. Britton, 24 Nov. 1923, SC.

15. F. Shreve, "The desert of northern Baja California," *Bulletin of the Torrey Botanical Club* 53 (1926): 132.

16. Ibid., 136.

17. Ibid., 135.

A Wider Outlook

1. MacDougal, who retired officially in 1933, continued to work at the Coastal Laboratory on the physiology of tree growth until 1939, when the Carnegie Institution sold the land and buildings.

2. F. Shreve to J. B. Overton, 11 Oct. 1929, SC.
3. H. A. Spoehr to F. Shreve, 19 March 1928, SC.
4. F. Shreve to H. A. Spoehr, 24 March 1928, SC.
5. F. Shreve to J. L. Wirt, 18 April 1929, SC.
6. J. C. Merriam, Confidential memorandum regarding difficult administrative situation, 24 Feb. 1929, CIW.
7. E. N. Transeau to F. Shreve, 10 April 1930, SC.
8. Arizona WPA Writers' Project, *Arizona: A State Guide* (New York: Hastings House, 1940), 253.
9. F. Shreve to E. B. Working, 18 Sept. 1930, SC.
10. F. Shreve, "The Desert Laboratory of the Carnegie Institution of Washington," *The Collecting Net* 6 (1931): 146.
11. F. Shreve to J. W. Shive, 14 June 1930, SC.
12. B. M. Duggar to F. Shreve, 2 Feb. 1929, SC.
13. F. Shreve to T. D. Mallery, 5 Feb. 1929, SC.
14. F. Shreve to W. S. Cooper, 17 May 1930, SC.
15. W. S. Cooper to F. Shreve, 28 May 1930, SC.
16. F. Shreve to W. J. Robbins, 20 Feb. 1933, SC.
17. F. Shreve to B. E. Livingston, 6 Oct. 1937, SC.
18. F. Shreve to H. A. Spoehr, 4 June 1937, SC.
19. W. V. Turnage, "Golden days at the Desert Laboratory" (1970), unpublished manuscript.
20. E. Ashby to J. E. Bowers, 27 Aug. 1984.
21. R. R. Humphrey to J. E. Bowers, 17 Aug. 1983.
22. R. R. Humphrey, personal communication, March 1986.
23. Interviews with M. S. Conn, 8 Oct. 1983; M. Denney, 17 Oct. 1983; H. S. Gentry, 19 April 1984; W. G. McGinnies, 26 Jan. 1984; and E. T. Nichols, 18 April 1984.

A Splendid Field for Work

1. F. V. Coville et al., *Carnegie Yearbook*, vol. 1, 1902 (Washington, D. C.: Carnegie Institution of Washington, 1903), 5.
2. F. Shreve, *Carnegie Yearbook*, vol. 30, 1930/1931 (Washington, D. C.: Carnegie Institution of Washington, 1931), 256.
3. F. Shreve to A. Killian, 15 Jan. 1930, SC.
4. James White, in "The census of plants in vegetation," in J. White, ed., *The Population Structure of Vegetation* (Dordrecht: Dr. W. Junk, 1985), 33–88, discusses the history of the Tumamoc Hill plots, as do D. E. Goldberg and R. M. Turner in "Vegetation change and plant demography in permanent plots in the Sonoran Desert," *Ecology* 67 (1986): 695–712.

5. Shreve, "Establishment of desert perennials," 216.
6. F. Shreve, "Changes in desert vegetation," *Ecology* 10 (1929): 370.
7. Ibid., 372.
8. Ibid., 372–73.
9. F. Shreve and A. L. Hinckley, "Thirty years of change in desert vegetation," *Ecology* 18 (1937): 478.
10. Goldberg and Turner, "Vegetation change and plant demography," 704.
11. F. Shreve to B. S. Meyer, 24 May 1929, SC.
12. Turnage, "Golden days," 10.
13. R. Daubenmire to J. E. Bowers, 2 April 1984.
14. F. Shreve to J. D. Laudermilk, 3 June 1930, SC.
15. F. Shreve to D. T. MacDougal, 27 May 1927, SC.
16. J. C. Merriam, Memorandum of conversation with Dr. Shreve, 5 Aug. 1930, CIW.
17. J. C. Merriam, Memorandum of conversation with Dr. Hall, 9 Sept. 1930, CIW.
18. H. A. Spoehr to F. Shreve, 29 Dec. 1931, SC.
19. F. Shreve to E. Huntington, 11 Feb. 1932, SC.
20. Shreve made this trip with H. Walter, L. R. Dice, W. P. Harris, and C. T. Vorhies.
21. F. Shreve to J. C. Merriam, 6 April 1932, SC.
22. R. R. Humphrey and I. L. Wiggins, in "Forrest Shreve: 1878–1950," *Science* 114 (1951): 569, state their belief that Shreve "felt impelled to work on projects initiated prior to his appointment as head of the Desert Laboratory before devoting his energies to the comprehensive survey of the desert vegetations." The evidence, however, suggests that Shreve did not conceive the Sonoran Desert project until 1932, four years after he took charge of the laboratory.
23. F. Shreve to J. C. Merriam, 30 April 1932, SC.
24. F. Shreve to D. S. Johnson, 5 Aug. 1932, SC.

Understanding Desert Life

1. F. Shreve to L. R. Abrams, 23 Jan. 1933, SC.
2. F. Shreve to J. C. Merriam, 30 Jan. 1933, SC.
3. Interview, W. G. McGinnies, 26 Jan. 1984.
4. T. D. Mallery, "More field trip episodes" (undated). Unpublished manuscript.
5. F. Shreve to B. Buttles, 14 July 1934, SC.
6. Interview, T. D. Mallery, 24 June 1984.

7. F. Shreve, "The desert and its life," *Carnegie Institution of Washington News Service Bulletin* no. 3 (Washington, D. C., 1934), 118.
8. T. D. Mallery to J. E. Bowers, 18 Aug. 1983.
9. Mallery, "More field trip episodes."
10. I. L. Wiggins to J. E. Bowers, 25 Sept. 1983.
11. H. A. Spoehr to F. Shreve, 22 Aug. 1934, SC.
12. F. Shreve to H. A. Spoehr, 30 Aug. 1934, SC.
13. F. Shreve, "Vegetation of the northwestern coast of Mexico," *Bulletin of the Torrey Botanical Club* 61 (1934): 379.
14. Ibid., 379–80.
15. F. Shreve to J. C. Merriam, 13 April 1933, SC.
16. F. Shreve to L. R. Abrams, 24 July 1934, SC.
17. F. Shreve to J. C. Merriam, 9 April 1934, SC.
18. F. Shreve, "The problems of the desert," *Scientific Monthly* 38 (1934): 208.
19. Ibid., 207.
20. F. Shreve to J. C. Merriam, 9 April 1934, SC.
21. F. Shreve to H. A. Spoehr, 15 Oct. 1934, SC.
22. F. Shreve to J. C. Merriam, 26 April 1935, SC.
23. Ibid.
24. F. Shreve, "The transition from desert to chaparral in Baja California," *Madroño* 3 (1936): 264.
25. Shreve, "Edge of the Desert," 11.
26. F. Shreve to J. C. Merriam, 11 April 1936, SC.
27. F. Shreve, "The plant life of the Sonoran Desert," *Scientific Monthly* 42 (1936): 213.
28. Ibid., 199.
29. Livingston and Shreve, *Distribution of Vegetation*, 19.
30. F. Shreve, *Carnegie Yearbook*, vol. 37, 1937/1938 (Washington, D. C.: Carnegie Institution of Washington, 1938), 224.
31. Shreve, "Plant life of the Sonoran Desert," 208.
32. F. Shreve to J. C. Merriam, 17 Feb. 1933, SC.
33. F. Shreve to J. C. Merriam, 20 July 1933, SC.
34. J. D. Laudermilk and P. A. Munz, "Plants in the dung of *Nothrotherium* from Gypsum Cave, Nevada," in *Contributions to Palaeontology IV*, Carnegie Institution of Washington Publication no. 453 (Washington, D. C., 1934), 29–37.
35. F. Shreve to E. Huntington, 13 Aug. 1934, SC.
36. F. Shreve to D. S. Johnson, 6 June 1935, SC.
37. F. Shreve (ca. 1938). Unpublished notes, UAH.
38. F. Shreve to P. C. Standley, 23 Sept. 1930, SC.
39. F. Shreve to W. M. Gilbert, 30 March 1937, SC.
40. F. Shreve to P. C. Standley, 3 March 1937, SC.

A Model and a Classic

1. F. Shreve to F. F. Bunker, 13 July 1934, SC.
2. *New York Herald Tribune*, 10 June 1934.
3. F. Shreve to F. F. Bunker, 13 July 1934, SC.
4. F. Shreve to D. T. MacDougal, 21 May 1935, SC.
5. F. Shreve to I. L. Wiggins, 17 July 1935, SC.
6. F. Shreve, "The plant resources of the Southwest" (1926), 10. Unpublished manuscript, SC.
7. Ibid., 12.
8. F. Shreve to E. R. Force, 23 July 1934, SC.
9. F. Shreve, Speech delivered to American Association for the Advancement of Science, Southwestern Division (ca. 1920). Unpublished manuscript, SC.
10. F. Shreve, *The Cactus and Its Home* (Baltimore: Williams & Wilkins, 1931), 29.
11. A. C. Gibson and P. S. Nobel, *The Cactus Primer* (Cambridge, Mass: Harvard University Press, 1986).
12. F. Shreve to S. A. Spear, 21 Jan. 1933, SC.
13. F. Shreve to A. I. Long, 10 Jan. 1933, SC.
14. C. T. Vorhies, "The Tucson Natural History Society," *Arizona Wild Life* 2 (1930): 8.
15. Shreve, "Plant resources," 14.
16. F. Shreve to J. C. Merriam, 25 Feb. 1932, SC.
17. F. Shreve to W. Seifriz, 23 March 1929, SC.
18. F. Shreve to P. C. Standley, 19 Jan. 1937, SC.
19. F. Shreve, memorandum, 24 Jan. 1944, UAH.
20. F. Shreve to C. L. Lundell, 21 Sept. 1935, SC.
21. L. Benson to P. S. Burgess, 5 Feb. 1944, UAH.
22. F. Shreve, *Carnegie Yearbook*, vol. 33, 1933/1934 (Washington, D. C.: Carnegie Institution of Washington, 1934), 189.
23. F. Shreve to J. C. Merriam, 11 April 1936, SC.
24. Internal evidence suggesting that Shreve wrote most of *Vegetation of the Sonoran Desert* in 1938 and 1939 includes the absence of citations to literature published after 1940.
25. Egler, "Forrest Shreve and the Sonoran Desert," 141.
26. F. Shreve, *Vegetation of the Sonoran Desert*, Carnegie Institution of Washington Publication no. 591 (Washington, D. C., 1951), 40.
27. Ibid., 49.
28. Ibid., 61.
29. Ibid., 72.
30. Ibid., 79.
31. C. H. Muller to J. E. Bowers, 18 May 1984.

32. A. G. Tansley, "The International Phytogeographic Excursion (I. P. E.) in America, 1913," *The New Phytologist* 13 (1913/1914): 328–29.

33. R. M. Turner and D. E. Brown, "Sonoran desertscrub," *Desert Plants* 4 (1982): 181.

34. Shreve, *Vegetation of the Sonoran Desert*, 87.

35. F. E. Clements, "The origin of the desert climax and climate," in T. H. Goodspeed, ed., *Essays in Geobotany in Honor of William Albert Setchell* (Berkeley: University of California Press, 1936), 88.

36. Shreve, *Vegetation of the Sonoran Desert*, 18.

37. Clements, *Plant Succession*, 34.

38. F. E. Clements, "The relict method in dynamic ecology," *Journal of Ecology* 22 (1934): 60.

39. F. Shreve to W. Seifriz, 31 Oct. 1929, SC.

40. Shreve, *Vegetation of the Sonoran Desert*, 21–22.

41. Ibid., 21.

42. F. Shreve, "The desert vegetation of North America," *Botanical Review* 8 (1942): 203–4.

43. S. E. Kingsland, in *Modeling Nature* (Chicago: University of Chicago Press, 1985), presents a detailed history of theoretical population ecology. In *The Background of Ecology* (Cambridge: Cambridge University Press, 1985), R. P. McIntosh provides a more compressed historical summary.

A Bitter Shock

1. F. Shreve to J. C. Merriam, 2 March 1937, SC.

2. F. Shreve to H. A. Spoehr, 9 Aug. 1937, SC.

3. F. Shreve, "Observations on the vegetation of Chihuahua," *Madroño* 5 (1939): 4–5.

4. Ibid., 13.

5. F. Shreve, *Carnegie Yearbook*, vol. 38, 1938/1939 (Washington, D. C.: Carnegie Institution of Washington, 1939), 128.

6. F. Shreve, *Carnegie Yearbook*, vol. 44, 1944/1945 (Washington, D. C.: Carnegie Institution of Washington, 1945), 85.

7. Ibid.

8. J. C. Merriam, Memorandum of conversation with Dr. Spoehr, 6 July 1934, CIW.

9. F. Shreve to H. A. Spoehr, 28 Aug. 1933, SC.

10. H. A. Spoehr to F. Shreve, 31 Aug. 1933, SC.

11. Interview, T. D. Mallery, 24 June 1984. During the interview Mallery read aloud the quoted portion of the letter, which he had copied from the original (apparently no longer extant) some years before.

12. F. Shreve to E. B. Working, 9 Jan. 1936, SC.

13. H. A. Spoehr to F. Shreve, 13 July 1937, SC.
14. Shreve, "The problems of the desert," 204.
15. V. Bush, *Carnegie Yearbook*, vol. 39, 1939/1940 (Washington, D. C.: Carnegie Institution of Washington, 1940), 7.
16. Shreve, "Desert vegetation of North America," 211.
17. Ibid., 196.
18. F. Shreve to P. Train, 19 Jan. 1937, SC.

Weaving the Threads

1. Shreve's research in the Sonoran Desert has laid the foundation for much of the later work done in the Southwest: R. H. Whittaker and W. A. Niering's gradient analysis of the Santa Catalina Mountains; W. F. Steenbergh and C. H. Lowe's study of saguaro ecology and demography; distribution maps of selected Sonoran Desert plants, prepared by J. R. Hastings, R. M. Turner, and D. K. Warren; R. R. Humphrey's study of the cirio; D. Axelrod's work on the origin of Sonoran Desert vegetation; and many more studies.
2. F. Shreve, "Ecological work at the Desert Laboratory" (ca. 1933), 15. Unpublished manuscript, SC.
3. Shreve, "Ecological work at the Desert Laboratory," 16.
4. Shreve, "Plant life of the Sonoran Desert," 213.
5. Shreve, *The Cactus and Its Home*, vi.
6. C. H. Muller to J. E. Bowers, 18 May 1984.
7. Humphrey and Wiggins, "Forrest Shreve: 1878–1950," 570.
8. Quoted in W. G. McGinnies, "The Desert Laboratory of the Carnegie Institution of Washington: History and Achievements" (1981). Unpublished manuscript, SC.

Bibliography

Arizona WPA Writers' Project. 1940. *Arizona: A State Guide*. New York: Hastings House.

Arrhenius, O. 1921. "Species and area." *Journal of Ecology* 9: 95–99.

Axelrod, D. I. 1979. *Age and Origin of Sonoran Desert Vegetation*. Occasional Papers of the California Academy of Sciences no. 132, San Francisco.

Billings, W. D. 1980. "American deserts and their mountains: An ecological frontier." *Bulletin of the Ecological Society of America* 61:203–9.

———. 1985. "The historical development of physiological plant ecology," in B. F. Chabot and H. A. Mooney, eds., *Physiological Ecology of North American Plant Communities*, 1–15. New York: Chapman and Hall.

Bowden, J. 1850. *The History of the Society of Friends in America*, vol. 1. London: Charles Gilpin; New York: Arno Press, 1972.

Bowers, J. E. 1983. "Jacob Corwin Blumer, Arizona botanist." *Brittonia* 35:197–203.

———. 1985. "The making of a flora for Arizona, 1901–1951, or why *Arizona Flora* is published by the University of California." *Desert Plants* 7:181–83, 211.

———. 1986. "A career of her own: Edith Shreve at the Desert Laboratory." *Desert Plants* 8:23–29.

Boyd, R. S., and G. D. Brum. 1983. "Postdispersal reproductive biology of a Mojave Desert population of *Larrea tridentata* (Zygophyllaceae)." *American Midland Naturalist* 110:25–36.

Brown, J. R. 1974. *Adventures in the Apache Country: A Tour Through Arizona and Sonora, 1864*. Tucson: University of Arizona Press.

Bufkin, D. 1981. "From mud village to modern metropolis: The urbanization of Tucson." *Journal of Arizona History* 22:63–98.

Burgess, R. L. 1977. "The Ecological Society of America: Historical data and some preliminary analyses," in F. N. Egerton and R. P. McIntosh, eds., *History of American Ecology*, 1–24. New York: Arno Press.

Cain, S. A. 1959. "Henry Allan Gleason, Eminent Ecologist 1959." *Bulletin of the Ecological Society of America* 40:105–10.

Carnegie Yearbook, vols. 1–39. 1902–1940. Washington, D. C.: Carnegie Institution of Washington.

Cittadino, E. 1980. "Ecology and the professionalization of botany in America, 1890–1902." *Studies in the History of Biology* 4:171–98.

Clements, F. E. 1905. *Research Methods in Ecology*. Lincoln, Nebraska: University Publishing Company.

———. 1907. *Plant Physiology and Ecology*. New York: Henry Holt & Co.

———. 1916. *Plant Succession*. Carnegie Institution of Washington Publication no. 242. Washington, D. C.

———. 1920. *Plant Indicators*. Carnegie Institution of Washington Publication no. 290. Washington, D. C.

———. 1934. "The relict method in dynamic ecology." *Journal of Ecology* 22:39–68.

———. 1936. "The origin of the desert climax and climate," in T. H. Goodspeed, ed., *Essays in Geobotany in Honor of William Albert Setchell*, 87–140. Berkeley: University of California Press.

Coker, W. C. 1937. "Professor Duncan Starr Johnson." *Science* 86:510–12.

Dean, J. M., and A. P. Smith. 1978. "Behavioral and morphological adaptations of a tropical plant to high rainfall." *Biotropica* 10:152–54.

"Dr. H. A. Gleason, distinguished ecologist." 1953. *Bulletin of the Ecological Society of America* 34:41

Doherty, R. W. 1967. *The Hicksite Separation*. New Brunswick: Rutgers University Press.

Eddington, A. S. 1929. *Science and the Unseen World*. New York: Macmillan.

Egler, F. E. 1951. "A commentary on American plant ecology, based on the textbooks of 1947–1949." *Ecology* 32:673–95.

———. 1954. "Forrest Shreve and the Sonoran Desert." *The Geographical Review* 44:137–41.

Ewan, J. A. 1971. "Clements, Frederic Edward," *Dictionary of Scientific Biography* 3:317–18. New York: Charles Scribner's Sons.

Fuller, G. D. 1915. "A montane rain-forest." *Botanical Gazette* 60:237–40.
Gibson, A. C., and P. S. Nobel. 1986. *The Cactus Primer*. Cambridge, Mass.: Harvard University Press.
Gleason, H. A. 1917. "The structure and development of the plant association." *Bulletin of the Torrey Botanical Club* 44:463–81.
———. 1922. "On the relation between species and area." *Ecology* 3:158–62.
———. 1926. "The individualistic concept of the plant association." *Bulletin of the Torrey Botanical Club* 53:7–26.
———. 1936. "Twenty-five years of ecology, 1910–1935." *Memoirs of the Brooklyn Botanical Garden* 4:41–49.
———. 1939. "The individualistic concept of the plant association." *American Midland Naturalist* 21:92–110.
———. 1975. "Delving into the history of American ecology." *Bulletin of the Ecological Society of America* 56:7–10.
Goldberg, D. E., and R. M. Turner. 1986. "Vegetation change and plant demography in permanent plots in the Sonoran Desert." *Ecology* 67:695–712.
Goodland, R. J. 1975. "The tropical origin of ecology: Eugen Warming's jubilee." *Oikos* 26:240–45.
Gould, S. J., and R. C. Lewontin. 1979. "The spandrels of San Marco and the Panglossian paradigm: A critique of the adaptationist programme." *Proceedings of the Royal Society of London B* 205:581–98.
Grover, S. C. 1981. *Toward a Psychology of the Scientist*. Washington, D. C.: University Press of America.
Grubb, P. J. 1977. "The maintenance of species-richness in plant communities: The importance of the regeneration niche." *Biological Review* 52:107–45.
Harper, J. L. 1967. "A Darwinian approach to plant ecology." *Journal of Ecology* 55:247–70.
Harper, K. T., D. C. Freeman, W. K. Ostler, and L. G. Klikoff. 1978. "The flora of Great Basin mountain ranges: Diversity, sources and dispersal ecology." *Great Basin Naturalist Memoirs* 2:81–103.
Hastings, J. R., R. M. Turner, and D. K. Warren. 1972. *An Atlas of Some Plant Distributions in the Sonoran Desert*. Technical Reports on the Meteorology and Climatology of Arid Regions no. 21. Tucson: Institute of Atmospheric Physics, University of Arizona.
Howard, R. A. 1961. "Ivan Murray Johnston, 1898–1960." *Journal of the Arnold Arboretum* 42:1–9.
Humphrey, H. B. 1961. "Forrest Shreve 1878–1950," in *Makers of North American Botany*, 230–31. New York: Ronald Press.

Humphrey, R. R. 1974. *The Boojum and Its Home*. Tucson: University of Arizona Press.

Humphrey, R. R., and I. L. Wiggins. 1951. "Forrest Shreve: 1878–1950." *Science* 114:569–70.

Johnson, D. S. 1914. "A montane rain forest." *Science* 40:897–98.

Karpiscak, M. M. 1980. "Secondary succession of abandoned field vegetation in southern Arizona." Ph.D. dissertation, University of Arizona.

Kearney, T. H., and R. H. Peebles. 1942. *Flowering Plants and Ferns of Arizona*. Washington, D. C.: USDA Miscellaneous Publication no. 423.

Kingsland, S. E. 1985. *Modeling Nature: Episodes in the History of Population Ecology*. Chicago: University of Chicago Press.

Laudermilk, J. D., and P. A. Munz. 1934. "Plants in the dung of *Nothrotherium* from Gypsum Cave, Nevada." *Contributions to Palaeontology IV*. Carnegie Institution of Washington Publication no. 453, 29–37. Washington, D. C.

Lawrence, D. B. 1948. "Introduction." *Ecology* 29:227–29.

Livingston, B. E. 1906. *The Relation of Desert Plants to Soil Moisture and to Evaporation*. Carnegie Institution of Washington Publication no. 50. Washington, D. C.

———. 1907. "Evaporation and plant development." *Plant World* 10:269–276.

———. 1908. "Evaporation and plant habitats." *Plant World* 11:1–9.

———. 1908. "Evaporation and centers of plant distribution." *Plant World* 11:106–12.

———. 1910. "Relation of soil moisture to desert vegetation." *Botanical Gazette* 50:241–56.

———. 1911. "A study of the relation between summer evaporation intensity and centers of plant distribution in the United States." *Plant World* 14:205–22.

———. 1913. "Climatic areas of the United States as related to plant growth." *American Philosophical Society, Proceedings* 52:257–75.

———. 1916. "Physiological temperature indices for the study of plant growth in relation to climatic conditions." *Physiological Researches* 1:399–420.

———. 1916. "A single index to represent both moisture and temperature conditions as related to plant growth." *Physiological Researches* 1:421–40.

———. 1948. "Some conversational autobiographical notes on intellectual experiences and development: An auto-obituary." *Ecology* 29:227–41.

Long, E. R. 1958. "Daniel Trembly MacDougal." *American Philosophical Yearbook* (1958): 131–35.

Lowe, C. H. 1961. "Biotic communities in the sub-Mogollon region of the inland Southwest." *Journal of the Arizona Academy of Science* 2:40–49.

MacArthur, R. H., and E. O. Wilson. 1967. *The Theory of Island Biogeography*. Princeton: Princeton University Press.

McAuliffe, J. R. 1984. "Sahuaro-nurse tree associations in the Sonoran Desert: Competitive effects of sahuaros." *Oecologia* 64:319–21.

———. 1986. "Herbivore-limited establishment of a Sonoran Desert tree, *Cercidium microphyllum*." *Ecology* 67:276–80.

MacDougal, D. T. 1908. *Botanical Features of North American Deserts*. Carnegie Institution of Washington Publication no. 99. Washington, D. C.

———. 1921. "The reactions of plants to new habitats." *Ecology* 2:1–20.

McGinnies, W. G. 1981. "The Desert Laboratory of the Carnegie Institution of Washington: History and achievements." Unpublished manuscript, Special Collections, University of Arizona Library.

———. 1981. *Discovering the Desert: Legacy of the Carnegie Desert Botanical Laboratory*. Tucson: University of Arizona Press.

McIntosh, R. P. 1974. "Plant ecology 1947–1972." *Annals of the Missouri Botanical Garden* 61:132–65.

———. 1975. "H. A. Gleason—'individualistic ecologist,' 1882–1975: His contributions to ecological theory." *Bulletin of the Torrey Botanical Club* 102:253–73.

———. 1976. "Ecology since 1900," in B. J. Taylor and T. J. White, eds., *Issues and Ideas in America*, 353–72. Norman: University of Oklahoma Press.

———. 1983. "Pioneer support for ecology." *BioScience* 33:107–12.

———. 1985. *The Background of Ecology: Concept and Theory*. Cambridge: Cambridge University Press.

MacMahon, J. A. 1980. "Ecosystems over time: Succession and other types of change," in R. H. Waring, ed., *Forests: Fresh Perspectives from Ecosystem Analysis*, 27–58. Corvallis: Oregon State University Press.

Maguire, B. 1975. "Henry Allan Gleason, January 2, 1882—April 21, 1975." *Bulletin of the Torrey Botanical Club* 102:274–77.

Martin, P. S. 1963. *The Last 10,000 Years*. Tucson: University of Arizona Press.

Mayr, E. 1982. *The Growth of Biological Thought*. Cambridge, Mass.: Harvard University Press, Belknap Press.

Merriam, C. H. 1894. "Laws of temperature control of the geographic distribution of terrestrial animals and plants." *National Geographic Magazine* 6:229–38.

Miller, A. A. 1950. *Climatology*, 7th ed. London: Methuen.

Moore, G. T., C. S. Gager, and F. Shreve. 1939. "Daniel Trembly MacDougal: Pioneer plant physiologist." *Plant Physiology* 14:191–202.

Muller, C. H. 1975. "Resolution of respect, Henry Allan Gleason, 1882–1975." *Bulletin of the Ecological Society of America* 56:25.

Parker, J. 1963. "Cold resistance in woody plants." *Botanical Review* 29:123–201.

Pool, R. J. 1954. "Frederic Edward Clements." *Ecology* 35:109–15.

Pound, R. 1954. "Frederic E. Clements as I knew him." *Ecology* 35:112–13.

Pound, R., and F. E. Clements. 1897. *Phytogeography of Nebraska*. Lincoln, Neb.: Botanical Seminar.

Raunkiaer, C. 1934. *The Life Forms of Plants and Statistical Plant Geography*. Oxford: Clarendon Press.

Reed, H. S. 1918. "Volney Morgan Spalding." *Plant World* 22: 14–18.

Reed, J. 1978. *From Private Vice to Public Virtue: The Birth Control Movement and American Society since 1830*. New York: Basic Books.

Robberecht, R., B. E. Mahall, and P. S. Nobel. 1983. "Experimental removal of intraspecific competitors—Effects on water relations and productivity of a desert bunchgrass, *Hilaria rigida*." *Oecologia* 60:21–24.

Rossiter, M. W. 1974. "Women scientists in America before 1920." *American Scientist* 62:312–23.

———. 1982. *Women Scientists in America: Struggles and Strategies to 1940*. Baltimore: Johns Hopkins University Press.

Rudolph, F. 1962. *The American College and University: A History*. New York: Knopf.

Schimper, A. F. W. 1903. *Plant-Geography Upon a Physiological Basis*. Oxford: Clarendon Press.

Shantz, H. L. 1951. "Forrest Shreve: 1878–1950." *Ecology* 32: 365–67.

Shelford, V. E. 1926. *The Naturalist's Guide to the Americas*. Baltimore: Williams & Wilkins.

Sheps, L. O. 1973. "Survival of *Larrea tridentata* seedlings in Death Valley National Monument, California." *Israel Journal of Botany* 22:8–17.

Shreve, E. B. 1914. *The Daily March of Transpiration in a Desert Perennial*. Carnegie Institution of Washington Publication no. 194. Washington, D. C.

———. 1915. "An investigation of the causes of autonomic movements in succulent plants." *Plant World* 18:297–312, 331–43.

———. 1916. "An analysis of the causes of variations in the transpiring power of cacti." *Physiological Researches* 2:73–127.

———. 1923. "Seasonal changes in the water relations of desert plants." *Ecology* 4:266–92.

———. 1924. "Factors governing seasonal changes in transpiration of *Encelia farinosa*." *Botanical Gazette* 77: 432–39.

———. 1940. "The relation of transpiration to evaporation from artificial surfaces." *American Journal of Botany* 27:707.

Sonnichsen, C. L. 1982. *Tucson: The Life and Times of an American City.* Norman: University of Oklahoma Press.

Spalding, V. M. 1909. *Distribution and Movements of Desert Plants.* Carnegie Institution of Washington Publication no. 113. Washington, D. C.

Spoehr, A., and H. S. Miller. 1956. *Essays on Science by Herman Augustus Spoehr: A Selection from His Works.* Stanford: Stanford University Press.

Sprugel, D. G. 1980. "A 'pedagogical genealogy' of American plant ecologists." *Bulletin of the Ecological Society of America* 61:197–200.

Steenbergh, W. F., and C. H. Lowe. 1977. *Ecology of the Saguaro: II. Reproduction, Germination, Establishment, Growth, and Survival of the Young Plant.* National Park Service Scientific Monograph Series no. 8. Washington, D. C.

———. 1983. *Ecology of the Saguaro: III. Growth and Demography.* National Park Service Scientific Monograph Series no. 17. Washington, D. C.

Steere, W. C. 1976. *Biological Abstracts/BIOSIS: The First Fifty Years.* New York: Plenum Press.

Stiles, W. 1954. "Dr. Herman A. Spoehr." *Nature* 174:534–35.

Storer, N. W. 1966. *The Social System of Science.* New York: Holt, Rinehart and Winston.

Sykes, G. 1944. *A Westerly Trend.* Tucson: Arizona Pioneers Historical Society. Reprinted by the University of Arizona Press, Tucson, 1985.

Tansley, A. G. 1913–14. "The International Phytogeographic Excursion (I. P. E.) in America, 1913." *The New Phytologist* 12:322–36; 13:30–41, 83–92, 268–75, 325–33.

———. 1947. "Frederic Edward Clements." *Journal of Ecology* 34:194–96.

Thornber, J. J., and F. Bonker. 1932. *The Fantastic Clan.* New York: Macmillan.

Thornthwaite, C. W. 1931. "The climates of North America according to a new classification." *Geographical Review* 21:633–55.

———. 1948. "An approach toward a rational classification of climate." *Geographical Review* 38:55–94.

Tobey, R. C. 1981. *Saving the Prairies: The Life Cycle of the Founding School of American Plant Ecology, 1895–1955.* Berkeley: University of California Press.

Tolles, F. B. 1948. *Meeting House and Counting House: The Quaker Merchants of Colonial Philadelphia, 1682–1763.* Chapel Hill: University of North Carolina Press.

———. 1960. *Quakers and the Atlantic Culture.* New York: Macmillan.

Transeau, E. N. 1905. "Climatic centers and centers of plant distribution." *Annual Report of the Michigan Academy of Science* 7:73–75.

———. 1905. "Forest centers of eastern North America." *American Naturalist* 39:875–89.

Turner, R. M., and D. E. Brown. 1982. "Sonoran desertscrub." *Desert Plants* 4:181–221.

Vandermeer, J. 1980. "Saguaros and nurse trees: A new hypothesis to account for population fluctuations." *Southwestern Naturalist* 25:357–60.

Van Devender, T. R., and W. G. Spaulding. 1979. "Development of vegetation and climate in the southwestern United States." *Science* 204:701–10.

Veysey, L. R. 1965. *The Emergence of the American University*. Chicago: University of Chicago Press.

Vorhies, C. T. 1930. "The Tucson Natural History Society." *Arizona Wild Life* 2:8, 25.

Webb, R. H., and H. G. Wilshire. 1980. "Recovery of soils and vegetation in a Mojave Desert ghost town, Nevada, U.S.A." *Journal of Arid Environments* 3:291–303.

Wells, P. V. 1961. "Succession in desert vegetation on streets of a Nevada ghost town." *Science* 134:670–71.

White, J. 1985. "The census of plants in vegetation," in J. White, ed., *The Population Structure of Vegetation*, 33–88. Dordrecht: Dr. W. Junk.

Whittaker, R. H. 1951. "A criticism of the plant association and climatic climax concepts." *Northwest Science* 25:17–31.

———. 1962. "Classification of communities." *Botanical Review* 28:1–239.

Whittaker, R. H., and W. A. Niering. 1965. "Vegetation of the Santa Catalina Mountains, Arizona: A gradient analysis of the south slope." *Ecology* 46:429–52.

Wilder, J. C. 1967. "The years of a desert laboratory." *Journal of Arizona History* 8:179–99.

Wilson, M. G. 1979. *The American Woman in Transition: The Urban Influence, 1870–1920*. Westport: Greenwood Press.

Publications of Forrest Shreve

1904. "Some plants which entrap insects." *Popular Science Monthly* 65:417–31.

1905. "The development of *Sarracenia purpurea* L." *Johns Hopkins University Circular* 1905(5):31–34.

1906. "A collecting trip at Cinchona." *Torreya* 6:81–84.

———. "The development and anatomy of *Sarracenia purpurea*." *Botanical Gazette* 42:107–26.

———. "The Hope Botanical Gardens." *Plant World* 9:201–7.
———. "A winter at the tropical station of the Garden." *Journal of the New York Botanical Garden* 7:193–96.
1907. "Studies on rate of growth in the mountain forests of Jamaica." *Johns Hopkins University Circular* 1907(3):31–37.
1908. "Transpiration and water storage in *Stelis ophioglossoides* Sw." *Plant World* 11:165–72.
1910. "The ecological plant geography of Maryland." *Maryland Weather Service* 3:101–48, 199–219, 275–92.
———. "The floristic plant geography of Maryland." *Maryland Weather Service* 3:69–97.
———. "The relation of natural vegetation to crop possibilities." *Maryland Weather Service* 3:295–303.
———. (with M. A. Chrysler, F. H. Blodgett, and F. W. Besley) *The Plant Life of Maryland*. Baltimore: Johns Hopkins University Press.
———. "The rate of establishment of the giant cactus." *Plant World* 13:235–40.
———. "The coastal deserts of Jamaica." *Plant World* 13:129–34.
1911. "Establishment behavior of the palo verde." *Plant World* 14:289–96.
———. "The influence of low temperature on the distribution of giant cactus." *Plant World* 14:136–46.
———. "Studies on Jamaican Hymenophyllaceae." *Botanical Gazette* 51:184–209.
1912. "Cold air drainage." *Plant World* 15:110–15.
———. (with B. E. Livingston) "The relation between climate and plant distributions in the United States." *Johns Hopkins University Circular* (1912):129–30.
1913. *A Guide to the Salient Physical and Vegetational Features of the Vicinity of Tucson*. Privately published.
1914. "The direct effects of rainfall on hygrophilous vegetation." *Journal of Ecology* 2:82–98.
———. *A Montane Rain-Forest: A Contribution to the Physiological Plant Geography of Jamaica*. Carnegie Institution of Washington Publication no. 199. Washington, D. C.
———. "The role of winter temperatures in determining the distribution of plants." *American Journal of Botany* 1:194–202.
———. "Rainfall as a determinant of soil moisture." *Plant World* 17:9–26.
1915. *The Vegetation of a Desert Mountain Range as Conditioned by Climatic Factors*. Carnegie Institution of Washington Publication no. 217. Washington, D. C.

1916. "Experimental work at Cinchona," in D. S. Johnson, "Cinchona as a tropical station for American botanists," *Science* 43:917–19.

———. "The weight of physical factors in the study of plant distribution." *Plant World* 19:53–67.

———. "Excursion impressions." *Transactions of the San Diego Society of Natural History* 2:79–83.

1917. "The density of stand and rate of growth of Arizona yellow pine as influenced by climatic conditions." *Journal of Forestry* 15:695–707.

———. "The establishment of desert perennials." *Journal of Ecology* 5:210–16.

———. "A map of the vegetation of the United States." *Geographical Review* 3:119–25.

———. "The physical control of vegetation in rain-forest and desert mountains." *Plant World* 20:135–41.

1918. "The Jamaican filmy ferns." *American Fern Journal* 8:65–71.

1919. "A comparison of the vegetational features of two desert mountain ranges." *Plant World* 22:291–307.

1920. "An account of the saguaro," in N. L. Britton and J. N. Rose, *The Cactaceae* 2:166. Carnegie Institution of Washington Publication no. 248. Washington, D. C.

1921. (with B. E. Livingston) *The Distribution of Vegetation in the United States as Related to Climatic Conditions*. Carnegie Institution of Washington Publication no. 284. Washington, D. C.

1922. "Conditions indirectly affecting vertical distribution on desert mountains." *Ecology* 3:269–74.

1924. "The growth record in trees," in D. T. MacDougal and F. Shreve, *Growth in Trees and Massive Organs of Plants*, 89–116. Carnegie Institution of Washington Publication no. 350. Washington, D. C.

———. "Across the Sonoran Desert." *Bulletin of the Torrey Botanical Club* 51:283–93.

———. "Soil temperature as influenced by altitude and slope exposure." *Ecology* 5:128–36.

1925. "Ecological aspects of the deserts of California." *Ecology* 6:93–103.

1926. "The Desert Laboratory." *Progressive Arizona* 3:10–11, 40.

———. (with D. T. MacDougal) "Can the primitive forest ever return?" *National Parks Bulletin* 49:11–12.

———. "The desert of northern Baja California." *Bulletin of the Torrey Botanical Club* 53:129–36.

1927. "The vegetation of a coastal mountain range." *Ecology* 8:27–44.

———. "The physical conditions of a coastal mountain range." *Ecology* 8:398–414.

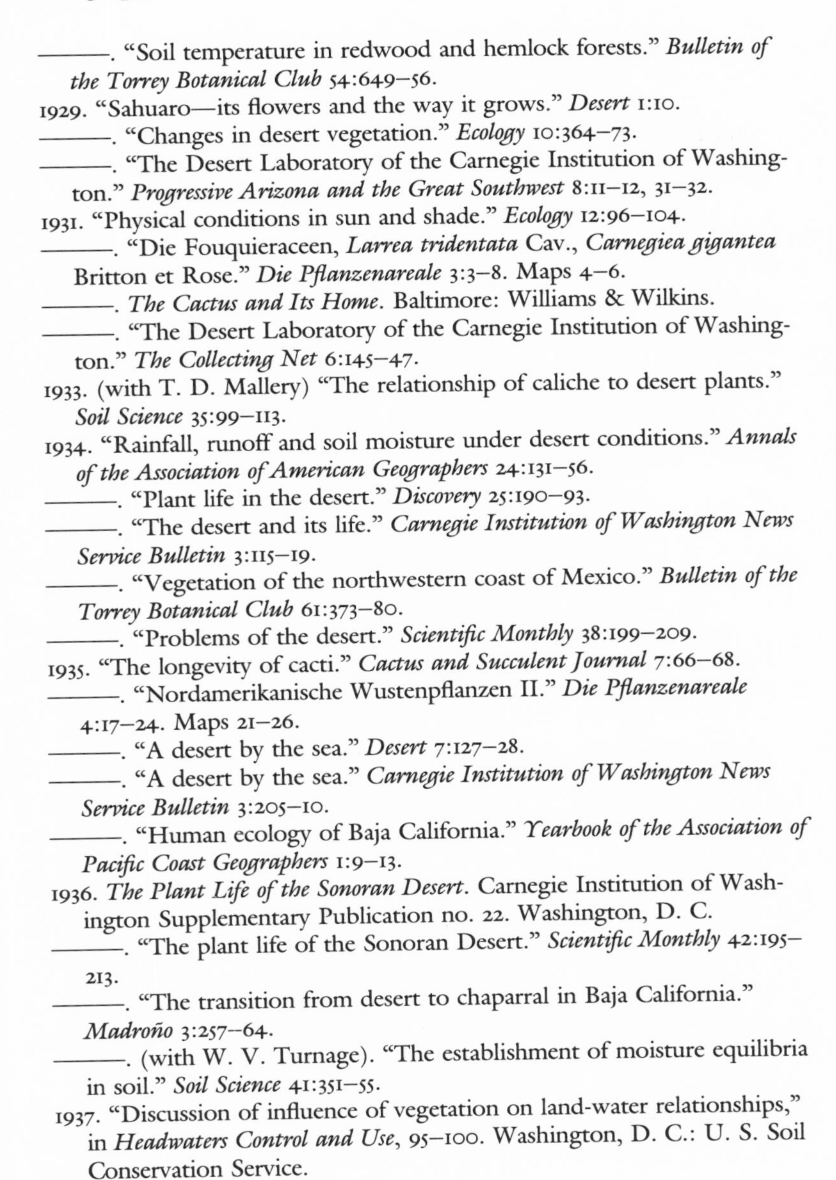

———. "Soil temperature in redwood and hemlock forests." *Bulletin of the Torrey Botanical Club* 54:649–56.
1929. "Sahuaro—its flowers and the way it grows." *Desert* 1:10.
———. "Changes in desert vegetation." *Ecology* 10:364–73.
———. "The Desert Laboratory of the Carnegie Institution of Washington." *Progressive Arizona and the Great Southwest* 8:11–12, 31–32.
1931. "Physical conditions in sun and shade." *Ecology* 12:96–104.
———. "Die Fouquieraceen, *Larrea tridentata* Cav., *Carnegiea gigantea* Britton et Rose." *Die Pflanzenareale* 3:3–8. Maps 4–6.
———. *The Cactus and Its Home*. Baltimore: Williams & Wilkins.
———. "The Desert Laboratory of the Carnegie Institution of Washington." *The Collecting Net* 6:145–47.
1933. (with T. D. Mallery) "The relationship of caliche to desert plants." *Soil Science* 35:99–113.
1934. "Rainfall, runoff and soil moisture under desert conditions." *Annals of the Association of American Geographers* 24:131–56.
———. "Plant life in the desert." *Discovery* 25:190–93.
———. "The desert and its life." *Carnegie Institution of Washington News Service Bulletin* 3:115–19.
———. "Vegetation of the northwestern coast of Mexico." *Bulletin of the Torrey Botanical Club* 61:373–80.
———. "Problems of the desert." *Scientific Monthly* 38:199–209.
1935. "The longevity of cacti." *Cactus and Succulent Journal* 7:66–68.
———. "Nordamerikanische Wustenpflanzen II." *Die Pflanzenareale* 4:17–24. Maps 21–26.
———. "A desert by the sea." *Desert* 7:127–28.
———. "A desert by the sea." *Carnegie Institution of Washington News Service Bulletin* 3:205–10.
———. "Human ecology of Baja California." *Yearbook of the Association of Pacific Coast Geographers* 1:9–13.
1936. *The Plant Life of the Sonoran Desert*. Carnegie Institution of Washington Supplementary Publication no. 22. Washington, D. C.
———. "The plant life of the Sonoran Desert." *Scientific Monthly* 42:195–213.
———. "The transition from desert to chaparral in Baja California." *Madroño* 3:257–64.
———. (with W. V. Turnage). "The establishment of moisture equilibria in soil." *Soil Science* 41:351–55.
1937. "Discussion of influence of vegetation on land-water relationships," in *Headwaters Control and Use*, 95–100. Washington, D. C.: U. S. Soil Conservation Service.

———. "Lowland vegetation of Sinaloa." *Bulletin of the Torrey Botanical Club* 64:605–13.
———. "Plants of the sand." *Carnegie Institution of Washington News Service Bulletin* 4:91–96.
———. "The vegetation of the Cape region of Baja California." *Madroño* 4:105–13.
———. (with A. L. Hinckley) "Thirty years of change in desert vegetation." *Ecology* 18:463–78.
1938. "The sandy areas of the North American desert." *Yearbook of the Association of Pacific Coast Geographers* 4:11–14.
1939. "Observations on the vegetation of Chihuahua." *Madroño* 5:1–13.
———. (with G. T. Moore and C. S. Gager) "Daniel Trembly MacDougal, pioneer plant physiologist." *Plant Physiology* 14:191–202.
1940. "The edge of the desert." *Yearbook of the Association of Pacific Coast Geographers* 6:6–11.
1942. "The life forms and flora of the North American desert." *Proceedings of the 8th American Scientific Congress, Washington, D. C., 1940* 3:125–32.
———. "Grassland and related vegetation in northern Mexico." *Madroño* 6:190–98.
———. "The desert vegetation of North America." *Botanical Review* 8:195–246.
———. "The vegetation of Jamaica." *Chronica Botanica* 7:164–66.
———. "Vegetation of northern Mexico." *Yearbook of the Association of Pacific Coast Geographers* 8:3–5.
———. "Vegetation of Arizona," in T. H. Kearney and R. H. Peebles, *Flowering Plants and Ferns of Arizona*, 10–23. U. S. Department of Agriculture Miscellaneous Publication no. 423. Washington, D. C.
1944. "Rainfall of northern Mexico." *Ecology* 25:105–11.
1945. "The saguaro, cactus camel of Arizona." *National Geographic Magazine* 88:695–704.
1951. *Vegetation of the Sonoran Desert*. Carnegie Institution of Washington Publication no. 591. Washington, D. C.
1964. "Vegetation of the Sonoran Desert," in F. Shreve and I. L. Wiggins. *Vegetation and Flora of the Sonoran Desert* 1:1–186. Stanford: Stanford University Press.

Index

Abrams, LeRoy, 108, 109
Acacia: farnesiana, 141; greggii, 40
Acclimatization, 20, 21, 49
"Across the Sonoran Desert," 89–90
Adaptation: morphological aspects of, 25–26, 119–20, 126–27, 137; to deserts, 100, 120, 127; to rain forests, 26, 119
Adaptationist programme, 26
Agave: 133, 141; *shrevei*, 128
Alpine Laboratory, 57, 91, 143
Ambrosia: deltoidea, 40, 102; *dumosa*, 86, 88, 132, 135; taxonomy of, 122
American Association for the Advancement of Science, 82, 86
Anatomy: plant, 6, 13, 26, 104, 110, 121; Shreve's attitude toward, 6–7, 110–11, 117
Arizona: as a scientific backwater, 2, 20, 107; Shreve's travels in, 46, 47–49, 64, 88, 115, 123, 128. *See also* Santa Catalina Mountains, fieldwork in
Artemisia tridentata, 86
Ashby, Eric, 98, 103–4, 107
Aspect. *See* Slope exposure
Atmometers, 20, 70–71
Atriplex hymenelytra, 121
Austin, Mary, 14
Automobiles, in fieldwork, 44–45, 111–12
Avra Valley, 104

Bailey, Irving W., 70, 94
Baja California, Shreve's travels in, 90, 112, 113, 114, 117–18
Barrel cactus, 36, 89, 120, 127, 132
Bartram, John, 4
Bartram, William, 4
Bellamy, Alfred David, 21
Bellamy, Edith Coffin. *See* Shreve, Edith B.
Bellamy, Leonora Coffin, 21
Benson, Lyman, 129
Besley, Fred W., 9
Bessey, Charles, 42
Biological Laboratory, Cold Spring Harbor, 14
Blackwelder, Eliot, 110
Blodgett, Frederich H., 9
Blossom, Philip, 107

Blue Mountains: comparison with Santa Catalina Mountains, 85–86; vegetation of, 12, 13–14, 26–30
Boojum tree, 89, 110, 125, 129
Botanical Abstracts (journal), 82
Botanical Society of America, 33, 46
Brittlebush, 40, 89, 102, 132
Britton, Nathaniel, 46, 122
Brongniartia shrevei, 128
Brown, David, 134
Bursage: taxonomy of, 122; triangle-leaf, 40, 102; white, 86, 88, 132, 135
Bursera, 89, 133
Bush, Vannevar, 145

Cacti, 46, 51, 110, 133; conservation of, 127, 128; evolution of, 121–22, 126–27; physiology of, 87, 126–27
Cactus and Its Home, The, 126–27
California, travels in, 69, 86, 125, 128
Calliandra eriophylla, 102
Cameron, A. E., 79
Cannon, William A., 15, 78
Cardón, 89
Carnegie Institution of Washington, 68, 94, 130; annual meeting, 113, 124–25; fiscal matters, 69, 106–7, 110, 113–14, 142–43, 145; goals of, 143, 145; personnel of, 57, 60, 93, 120, 145; research stations, 15–16, 82. *See also* Alpine Laboratory; Coastal Laboratory; Desert Laboratory
Carnegie Yearbook (annual report), 83, 104, 141
Carnegiea gigantea. *See* Saguaro.
Catclaw, 40
Century plant, 133, 141
Cercidium. *See* Palo verde, blue; Palo verde, little-leaf
Chaney, Ralph W., 94, 110
"Changes in Desert Vegetation," 102–3
Chaparral, 84, 85, 118, 119
Chihuahuan Desert, 146; physiography of, 139; project, 138–39, 141, 145; subdivisions of, 139, 141; travels in, 138–39, 141, 145; vegetation of, 74, 139, 141
Cholla, 132
Chrysler, Mintin A., 9
Cinchona research station, 11, 12, 13, 21, 24, 30
Cirio, 89, 110. *See also* Boojum tree.
Clements, Edith, 42, 57
Clements, Frederic E., 8, 41, 42; at the Desert Laboratory, 57; education of, 56; influence on ecological thought, 56, 57–59, 62, 73, 103; Livingston's opinion of, 59; personality of, 55, 59, 60; Shreve's opinion of, 33, 55, 59–60; teaching career of, 56–57. Works: "Origin of the Desert Climax and Climate, The," 134; *Plant Physiology and Ecology*, 10; *Plant Succession*, 55; *Research Methods in Ecology*, 10, 56
Climate, and vegetation: in the Chihuahuan Desert, 141; in Jamaica, 13–14, 27–30; in the Santa Catalina Mountains, 50, 52–54; in the Santa Lucia Mountains, 84–86; in the Sonoran Desert, 90, 114–15, 117, 132–33, 136; in the United States, 75–76
Climatic change, 54, 64, 65–66, 102–3, 120–21
Climatic data, collection of, 13, 27, 49, 52, 70–71, 72, 75, 79
Climatic indices, 52–53, 71, 76, 135
Climax, 57, 58, 135–36; as defined by Clements, 11, 29; as defined by Shreve, 135–36; Shreve's rejection of, 29
"Coastal Deserts of Jamaica, The," 29–30
Coastal Laboratory, 31, 82, 84, 91
Cold-air drainage, 36, 38, 51
Coldenia, 102
"Collecting Trip at Cinchona, A," 14
Collection, plant, 45–46, 97, 108, 128–29
Colorado Desert, 72, 116
Committee on Scientific Research, 68
Communities, plant: as defined by Clements, 41, 57, 58; in the Chihuahuan Desert, 141; in Jamaica, 27–30; in Maryland, 10–11; in the

Santa Catalina Mountains, 51; in the Santa Lucia Mountains, 85; in the Sonoran Desert, 132–33, 134; in the United States, 74
Community ecology: defined, 12. *See also* Communities, plant; Vegetation
"Comparison of the Vegetational Features of Two Desert Mountain Ranges, A," 65
Competition: among desert plants, 35–36, 40–41; in humid regions, 36, 40, 119–20; Shreve's rejection of, 36, 40–41, 50, 54, 86, 120, 134
Competitive exclusion principle, 35–36, 136
Conservation. *See* Desert, conservation of
Continuum concept: defined, 29; in deserts, 133–34; general acceptance of, 58, 61, 149; in Jamaica, 29, 54; in the Midwest, 60–61; in the Santa Catalina Mountains, 54
Cooper, William S., 96
Cotton, 104
Coville, Frederick V., 8, 94
Cowles, Henry C., 8, 78
Creosote bush, 86, 87, 130, 132, 135; establishment of, 36, 103; physiology of, 15–16, 104
Crocker, Dr. (researcher from Chicago), 42
Cucopa Mountains, 90
Cuyamaca Mountains, 71–72

"Daily March of Transpiration in a Desert Perennial, The," (Edith Shreve), 66
Darwin, Charles, 33
Daubenmire, Rexford, 105
Demography, plant. *See* Population ecology
Denney, Marjorie, 98
Department of Botanical Research, 15, 16, 31, 69. *See also* Desert Laboratory
Depression, 106–8, 113–14, 143, 145
Descriptive ecology, 101, 108, 137
Desert: coastal, 29–30; commercial development of, 125–26; conservation of, 127–28; definitions of, 133–35; delineation of, 74–75, 76, 116, 123, 146; history of, 108, 117, 119; Old World, 133
Desert Laboratory, 21, 36, 46, 72, 81; administration of, 82–83, 91, 93–95, 144–45; atmosphere at, 42–43, 97–98; buildings and grounds of, 15, 43–44, 95; closing of, 141–45; conference on, 94; founding of, 15; mission of, 15, 94–95, 96, 100, 144–45; permanent plots at, 101–3; personnel of, 15–16, 31, 42–43, 57, 96–98, 105–6, 142–43; public relations of, 124–25; in the summer, 31, 84; thirtieth anniversary of, 142; vegetation at, 15, 101–2, 133, 145; visiting investigators at, 15–16, 42, 43, 98, 101, 103, 106–7
"Desert of Northern Baja California, The," 90
Desert Region, 51, 52, 53, 64
"Desert Vegetation of North America, The," 146
Desertscrub. *See* Chihuahuan Desert, vegetation of; Mojave Desert, vegetation of; Sonoran Desert, vegetation of
Development. *See* Desert, commercial development of
Dice, L. R., 138
Die Pflanzenareale (journal), 122, 130
"Direct Effects of Rainfall on Hygrophilous Vegetation, The," 26
Dispersal, plant, 65–66
Distribution, species: floristic aspects of, 9–10, 63–64, 72, 87, 115, 118; and moisture, 10, 52–53, 75–76, 122; and soil type, 104; and temperature, 38, 40, 46, 53, 75–76. *See also* Limiting factors
Distribution, vegetation. *See* Climate, and vegetation; Soil, and vegetation
Distribution of Vegetation in the United States as Related to Climatic Conditions, The, 71, 75–77
Diversity, species, 86, 115, 119, 132

Division of Plant Biology, 91, 106
Doughty, Jesse, 106
Drip-tips, 26
Drought tolerance, 103, 104, 115
Drude, Oscar, 7, 120
Duggar, Benjamin, 96
Dunes, 8, 41, 88

East Coast: as scientific center, 2, 20; trips to, 21, 46, 63, 70, 113
"Ecological Aspects of the Deserts of California," 86–87
Ecological Society of America: founding of, 78; growth of, 78–80; takes over *The Plant World*, 80–81
Ecology: coining of, 7; defined, 8; history of, 7–8, 12–13, 15. *See also* Community ecology; Descriptive ecology; Ecosystem ecology; Evolutionary ecology; Experimental ecology; Physiological ecology; Population ecology; Theoretical ecology
Ecology (journal), 73, 77, 81
Ecosystem ecology, 116–17, 144
"Edge of the Desert, The," 119, 137
Egler, Frank E., 58, 130
Elephant tree, 89, 133
Encelia farinosa, 40, 89, 102, 132
Encinal Region, 51, 52, 53, 64
Encino, 51
Ephedra, 88
Eriogonum, 122
Establishment: of creosote bush, 103; of desert perennials, 36, 101–3; of little-leaf palo verde, 34–35; of saguaro, 34
"Establishment Behavior of the Palo Verde," 34–35
Evaporation, 20, 70–71, 134–35
Evaporimeters. *See* Atmometers
Evolution, 119–20, 121–22, 126–27, 149
Evolutionary ecology, 117; defined, 12
Experimental ecology, 12–13, 24–26, 29, 73
Exposure. *See* Slope exposure

Fairy duster, 102
Ferocactus, 36, 89, 120, 127, 132
Fieldwork: difficulties of, 48–49, 111–13. *See also* Sonoran Desert project, field trips for; Travel
Financial crisis. *See* Carnegie Institution of Washington, fiscal matters
Fitting (professor from Bonn), 42
Flora: of Maryland, 9; of the Mojave Desert, 69; of the Santa Catalina Mountains, 63–64; of the Sonoran Desert, 108, 109, 115, 117, 132; of southern California, 72
Floristics. *See* Distribution, species
Flow, surface and underground, 53
Flowering Plants and Ferns of Arizona (Kearney and Peebles), 146
Forest Region, 51, 52, 53, 64
Formation. *See* Climax
Fossils, plant, 66, 120–21
Fouquieria: 110; *macdougalii*, 129; *shrevei*, 128. *See also* Ocotillo
Franseria. *See Ambrosia*
Free, Edward E., 69
Freezing. *See* Temperature, low
Funding. *See* Carnegie Institution of Washington, fiscal matters; Depression

Galleta, big, 41, 88
Gause, G. F., 35, 136
Gentry, Howard Scott, 97, 98, 148
Geography, plant. *See* Distribution, species
Germination: of desert ephemerals, 130; of desert perennials, 34, 35, 36, 87, 129; of little-leaf palo verde, 34–35
Gilbert, W. M., 124
Gleason, Henry A., 54; education of, 60; influence on ecological thought, 60–61, 136; teaching career of, 60
Goucher College. *See* Woman's College, The
Gould, Stephen J., 26
Gradient analysis: defined, 50; of the

Santa Catalina Mountains, 50–51, 52–53; of the Santa Lucia Mountains, 83
Grassland, 41, 84, 85
"Grassland and Related Vegetation in Northern Mexico," 137, 146
Grazing, effects of, 15, 101–2
Great Basin Desert, 64, 74, 146
Grubb, P. J., 35
Gulf of California, 88, 89, 112
Gypsum Cave, 121

Haeckel, Ernst, 7
Hall, Harvey M., 94
Harris, J. A., (visiting investigator), 43
Harshberger, John W., 8, 78
Herbarium: establishment of, 45–46; maintenance of, 128–29
Heredity, 21
Hilaria rigida, 41, 88
Hinckley, Arthur L., 96, 97, 102, 148
Holistic research. *See* Ecosystem ecology
Holly, desert, 121
Hornaday, William T., 88
Humboldt, Alexander von, 7
Humphrey, Robert R., 96–97, 101, 142
Huntington, Ellsworth, 69

Identification, plant, 45, 128
Idria columnaris, 89, 110, 125, 129
"Individualistic Concept of the Plant Association, The," (Gleason), 61
"Influence of Low Temperature on the Distribution of Giant Cactus, The," 39–40
International Botanical Congress, 61, 148
Ironwood, 129, 132
Island biogeography, 66

Jamaica: rainfall in, 27, 30; topography of, 28, 29; travel in, 26–27, 30; vegetation of, 12, 13–14, 27–29, 30
Jatropha cinerea, 133
Johns Hopkins University, 5–6, 12, 31, 66
Johnson, Duncan S., 6, 11, 110, 148
Johnston, Ivan M., 139, 141
Jones, Marcus E., 129
Joshua tree, 86, 121

Kearney, Thomas H., 7, 146
Keck, David, 119
Keddington, Mrs. (secretary), 93
Kraus, E. J., 107, 110

Larrea tridentata. *See* Creosote bush
Laudermilk, J. D., 121
Lawrence, D. B., 73
Laws, plant protection, 127
Lemaireocereus thurberi, 129, 132
Lewontin, R. C., 26
Life forms: in deserts, 119–20, 134; in rain forests, 29, 119–20
Life zones, 71–72, 77
Limber bush, 133
Limiting factors: moisture, 38, 52–53, 76, 87, 115, 118; temperature, 38, 40, 53, 115, 118
Liriodendron tulipifera, 75
Livingston, Burton E., 94; as business manager of *The Plant World*, 32; collaboration with Shreve, 70–71, 72, 75–77; death of, 148; as Edith Shreve's mentor, 23, 46, 66, 70; as editor, 59, 82; influence on Shreve, 73; personality of, 73; research of, 16, 76–77, 79; Shreve's influence on, 76–77; teaching career of, 31, 73
Lloyd, Francis E., 16
Lophocereus schottii, 129, 132
Lotka, A. J., 136
"Lowland Vegetation of Sinaloa," 137

MacDougal, Daniel T., 78, 142, 148; attitude toward Clements, 55, 56–57; becomes director of Desert Laboratory, 15, 16; as business manager of *The Plant World*, 32; as Edith Shreve's mentor, 23; establishes Coastal Laboratory, 31; personality of, 14, 33; relations with Woodward,

47–48, 84, 128; cold-air drainage in, 36, 38; comparison with Blue Mountains, 85–86; comparison with Pinaleno Mountains, 46, 64–65; comparison with Santa Lucia Mountains, 85–86; fieldwork in, 48–49; flora of, 63–65; gradient analysis of, 50–51, 52–53; vegetation of, 51–53
Santa Lucia Mountains, 83; gradient analysis of, 85; vegetation of, 84–85
Sarracenia purpurea, 6, 7
Schimper, A. F. W., 7, 12, 13
Schratz, Eduard, 107
Seedlings, survival of, 34, 35, 36, 40
Senita, 129, 132
Sequoia sempervirens, 85
Shantz, Homer L., 78
Shelford, Victor, 78, 79, 82
Shreve, Edith, 148; education of, 21; health of, 82; as a housewife, 30, 67, 95; marriage of, 21, 22–23, 30, 66–67; research of, 21, 22, 23, 66–67, 70, 82; teaching career of, 21
Shreve, Forrest: as an administrator, 82–83, 93–95, 98–99, 106; arrival in Tucson, 17, 18–19, 47, 149–50; attitude toward Clementsian ecology, 10–11, 28, 29, 33, 41, 50, 59–60, 85, 86, 87–88, 103, 135; attitude toward descriptive ecology, 101, 108; attitude toward women, 22–23; birth of, 4; childhood of, 4; collaboration with Livingston, 70–71, 72, 73–74, 76–77; committee work of, 68, 78, 81–82; as a conservationist, 125–26, 127–28; considers Forest Service position, 70; contributes to *Botanical Abstracts*, 82; daily routine of, 91, 98; death of, 148; dress of, 18, 98–99; edits *The Plant World*, 32–33, 80–81; education of, 4–6; evaluation of, 2, 29, 77, 130; first visits Sonora, 88; health of, 98, 113, 141, 148; herbarium of, 45–46, 128–29; hired by MacDougal, 16–17; impressions of the desert, 1, 150; influence on ecological thought, 2–3, 20, 33–34, 41, 54–55, 61–62, 73, 77; Livingston's influence on, 73; marriage of, 21, 22–23, 30, 66–67; Merriam's discontent with, 93–94, 106, 142, 143–44; offices held, 77, 78–80, 81–82, 127, 146, 148; philosophy of research, 2–3, 4, 101, 108, 116–17, 143–44, 149, 151; as a photographer, 111; as a politician, 99, 114, 142–43, 145; productivity of, 83; promotions of, 82–83, 91, 96; Quaker influence on, 4, 22–23, 26, 61–62, 98; relations with Spoehr, 93, 143; reputation of, 2, 77, 81; residences of, 43–44, 95; resists Ecological Society journal, 80–81; retirement of, 141, 148; Schimper's influence on, 13; teaching duties of, 14, 70; visits Jamaica, 11, 12, 21, 24; war activities of, 68–69. Works: "Across the Sonoran Desert," 89–90; *Cactus and Its Home, The*, 126–27; "Changes in Desert Vegetation," 102–3; "Coastal Desert of Jamaica, The," 29–30; "Collecting Trip at Cinchona, A," 14; "Comparison of the Vegetational Features of Two Desert Mountain Ranges, A," 65; "Desert of Northern Baja California, The," 90; "Desert Vegetation of North America, The," 146; "Direct Effects of Rainfall on Hygrophilous Vegetation, The," 26; *Distribution of Vegetation in the United States as Related to Climatic Conditions, The*, 71, 75–77; "Ecological Aspects of the Deserts of California," 86–87; "Edge of the Desert, The," 119, 137; "Establishment Behavior of the Palo Verde," 34–35; "Grassland and Related Vegetation in Northern Mexico," 137, 146; "Influence of Low Temperatures on the Distribution of Giant Cactus, The," 39–40; "Lowland Vegetation in Sinaloa," 137; *Montane Rain Forest, A*, 29, 50; *Naturalist's Guide to the Americas,*

The, 82; "Observations on the Vegetation of Chihuahua," 137; "Physical Conditions of a Coastal Mountain Range, The," 84–85; *Plant Life of Maryland, The*, 8, 9–11, 21; "Plant Life of the Sonoran Desert," 119–20; "Problems of the Desert, The," 116–17; "Rainfall as a Determinant of Soil Moisture," 39; "Rate of Establishment of the Giant Cactus, The," 34; "Relationship of Caliche to Desert Plants, The," 104; "Role of Winter Temperatures in Determining the Distribution of Plants, The," 46; "Soil Temperature in Redwood and Hemlock Forests," 84; "Some Plants Which Entrap Insects," 7; "Thirty Years of Change in Desert Vegetation," 102; "Transition from Desert to Chaparral in Baja California, The," 118; "Vegetation of a Coastal Mountain Range, The," 84–85; "Vegetation of Arizona, The," 146; *Vegetation of Desert Mountain Range as Conditioned by Climatic Factors*, 2, 38, 46, 49–55; "Vegetation of the Cape Region of Baja California," 137; "Vegetation of the Northwest Coast of Mexico," 114–15; *Vegetation of the Sonoran Desert*, 2, 103, 130–33, 134, 135, 136, 138
Shreve, Helen Garrison Coates (mother), 4–5
Shreve, Henry (father), 4
Shreve, Margaret (daughter), 22, 82
Shreve, Rachel Coates (grandmother), 3
Shreve, Solomon (grandfather), 3
Slope exposure, 53, 104
Sloth, ground, 120, 121
Soil: moisture of, 38–39, 51, 52–53, 86, 104–5; temperature of, 36, 51, 79, 104, 105, 129; and vegetation, 10, 30, 104, 132, 133, 139, 141
"Soil Temperatures in Redwood and Hemlock Forests," 84
"Some Plants Which Entrap Insects," 7
Sonora, travels in, 88, 89, 128. *See also* Sonoran Desert project, field trips for
Sonoran Desert: compared with Chihuahuan Desert, 138, 139, 141; delineation of, 74, 116, 118, 132–33, 146; flora of, 108, 109, 115, 117, 132; physiography of, 119, 130, 133, 135; subdivisions of, 116, 125, 132–33, 134, 135; vegetation of, 114–15, 117–19, 132–33, 134. *See also* Desert, history of
Sonoran Desert project: field trips for, 108, 109, 111–13, 114–16, 117–18, 119, 123; origin of, 108; research plans for, 110–11, 117
Spalding, Effie, 16, 19, 34
Spalding, Volney M., 15; edits *The Plant World*, 31–32; health of, 19, 31; research of, 19, 101, 103
Spoehr, Herman A., 69; as an administrator, 93, 106–7, 142; attitude toward Shreve, 142–43; hired by MacDougal, 31; promotions of, 82, 91; research of, 93, 143
Standley, Paul C., 45, 123
Stock, Chester, 120
Stokes, Susan, 122
Subclimax, 87, 135
Succession, 57, 58; competitive aspects of, 41; defined, 11, 88; in deserts, 87–88, 102, 103, 135–36; Shreve's rejection of, 87–88, 102, 103, 135–36
Swingle, W. T., 94
Sykes, Gilbert, 90
Sykes, Godfrey, 44, 69, 90, 101

Tansley, Arthur G., 57, 133
Taxonomy, plant: of bursage, 122; Shreve's attitude toward, 45–46, 122
Taylor, Walter P., 127
Temperature, 71, 76; high, 127; low, 38, 39–40, 46, 53, 90, 115, 127; nighttime, 38. *See also* Limiting factors, temperature; Soil, temperature of
Terminology, 10–11, 57, 88
Theoretical ecology, 61, 136

"Thirty Years of Change in Desert Vegetation," 102
Thornber, John James, 45, 63, 126, 142
Thornscrub, 114, 117, 132, 134
Tobey, Ronald C., 58
Toll, Roger, 128
Topography. *See* Relief, topographic
Torchwood, 133
Tower, William L. (visiting investigator), 43
Train, Percy, 146
Transeau, Edgar N., 8, 32, 71, 94
"Transition from Desert to Chaparral in Baja California, The," 118
Transitions, vegetational. *See* Vegetation, transitions in
Transpiration, 66; of rainforest plants, 13, 25
Transplant experiments, 20–21, 49
Travel: in Arizona, 46, 47–49, 64, 88, 115, 123, 128; in Baja California, 90, 112, 113, 114, 117–18; in California, 69, 86, 125, 128; in the Chihuahuan Desert, 138–39, 141, 145; difficulties in, 44–45, 48, 88–89, 111–12, 139; ease of, 111, 123; to the East Coast, 21, 46, 63, 70, 113; expenses of, 108, 114; by horseback, 27, 30, 48; to Jamaica, 11, 12, 21, 24; mileage, 111, 116, 130; in the Mojave Desert, 46, 69, 71–72, 86, 123; in Nevada, 115, 123; in New Mexico, 46; in Sonora, 88, 89, 128. *See also* Sonoran Desert project, field trips for
Tucson: described, 18–19, 95, 125; Shreve arrives in, 18, 19, 47, 150
Tucson Natural History Society, 127–28
Tulip tree, 75
Tumamoc Hill, 91; as a nature preserve, 15, 145; physiography of, 15; research at, 35, 39, 101, 103, 104. *See also* Desert Laboratory
Turnage, William V., 96, 97, 104–5, 113, 148
Turner, Raymond M. 134

Underwood, Lucien M., 11
U.S. Forest Service, 70, 74, 98, 128, 145

Vegetation: of the Avra Valley, 104; of the Blue Mountains, 12, 13–14, 26–29; changes in, 64, 65–66, 87–88, 101–3; of the Chihuahuan Desert, 139, 141; classification of, 10–11, 28–29, 51–52, 57, 58, 71–72, 74, 85, 118, 132, 135, 146; and climatic change, 65–66, 121; of the Cucopa Mountains, 90; of the Desert Laboratory, 15, 101–3; of the Jamaican coast, 30; of Maryland, 9–10; of the Mojave Desert, 86–87; of the Santa Catalina Mountains, 51–53; of the Santa Lucia Mountains, 84–85; of the Sonoran Desert, 114–15, 117–19, 132–33, 134; transitions in, 114–15, 118–19, 132, 134, 146. *See also* Climate, and vegetation; Communities, plant; Soil, and vegetation
"Vegetation of a Coastal Mountain Range, The," 84–85
Vegetation of a Desert Mountain Range as Conditioned by Climatic Factors, 2, 38, 46, 49–55
"Vegetation of Arizona, The," 146
"Vegetation of the Cape Region of Baja California, The," 137
"Vegetation of the Northwest Coast of Mexico," 114–15
Vegetation of the Sonoran Desert, 2, 103, 130–33, 134, 135, 136, 138
Villa, Pancho, 88
Visiting investigators. See Desert Laboratory, visiting investigators

Walter, Heinrich, 107
Warming, Eugen, 7, 12
Weather data. *See* Climatic data, collection of; Evaporation; Rainfall; Temperature
Weese, A. O., 80
Wheeler, William M., 78
Whitehead, Jack, 113
Whittaker, Robert H., 50, 51, 58, 64
Wiggins, Ira L., 109, 113, 114, 118, 128, 130
Woman's College, The, 14, 21, 71

Woodward, Robert, 69, 143
Wooton, E. O., 45
Working, Earl, 107
World War I, 67, 68–69, 79–80
World War II, 122, 130, 141

Yucca, 133, 141
Yucca brevifolia, 86, 121

About the Author

Janice Emily Bowers, botanist and writer, has worked for the U.S. Geological Survey since 1982, stationed at the Desert Laboratory on Tumamoc Hill in Tucson. She has prepared floras of Organ Pipe Cactus National Monument, Tumamoc Hill, and the Rincon Mountains. She is the author of *Seasons of the Wind: A Naturalist's Look at the Plant Life of Southwestern Sand Dunes* and *100 Roadside Wildflowers of Southwest Woodlands*, and she has published in journals such as *Ecology, Brittonia, Madroño, Great Basin Naturalist, Journal of Arid Environments*, and *Desert Plants*.